PEOPLE
PLEASER

PEOPLE PLEASER

Breaking Free from the Burden
of Imaginary Expectations

JINGER DUGGAR VUOLO

W PUBLISHING GROUP

AN IMPRINT OF THOMAS NELSON

Published in Nashville, Tennessee, by W Publishing, an imprint of Thomas Nelson.

The author is represented by Alive Literary Agency.

Thomas Nelson titles may be purchased in bulk for educational, business, fundraising, or sales promotional use. For information, please email SpecialMarkets@ThomasNelson.com.

Unless otherwise noted, Scripture quotations are taken from the ESV® Bible (The Holy Bible, English Standard Version®). Copyright © 2001 by Crossway, a publishing ministry of Good News Publishers. Used by permission. All rights reserved.

Scripture quotations marked NIV are taken from The Holy Bible, New International Version®, NIV®. Copyright © 1973, 1978, 1984, 2011 by Biblica, Inc.® Used by permission of Zondervan. All rights reserved worldwide. www.Zondervan.com. The "NIV" and "New International Version" are trademarks registered in the United States Patent and Trademark Office by Biblica, Inc.®

Any internet addresses, phone numbers, or company or product information printed in this book are offered as a resource and are not intended in any way to be or to imply an endorsement by Thomas Nelson, nor does Thomas Nelson vouch for the existence, content, or services of these sites, phone numbers, companies, or products beyond the life of this book.

ISBN 978-1-4003-4177-1 (audiobook)
ISBN 978-1-4003-4176-4 (ePub)
ISBN 978-1-4003-4748-3 (ITPE)
ISBN 978-1-4003-4171-9 (HC)

Library of Congress Control Number: 2024938945

Printed in the United States of America
24 25 26 27 28 LBC 5 4 3 2 1

To those wanting to be set free from the
bondage of everyone else's expectations:
"For freedom Christ has set us free." Galatians 5:1

To my mom, you will always be my hero
and best friend. I love you.

CONTENTS

CONTENTS

INTRODUCTION

HI.

I'm Jinger, also known as Jing to my husband and friends.

Someone once asked me, if my name wasn't Jinger, what would I want it to be? I responded that I love my name, that there's not another name I would want, and that I think it fits me perfectly. It's unique, original, with a little bit of spice. I like it.

I was born into a family that seemed perfectly normal to me, the sixth kid in the lineup, a family that would ultimately grow to a total of nineteen children. Even though I knew my family was a little unusual and stood out in my Arkansas hometown, my parents made a point of us spending time with a lot of other big families, families who also needed a fifteen-passenger van to get to the grocery store, families where the kids were stacked into rows upon rows of bunk beds at night, families who looked and talked and dressed and homeschooled a whole lot like mine. Granted, we put a lot of effort and time into being with these other families, attending conferences and events. But they were what I saw as the norm, families who were living life like my family was. The same.

It wasn't until I was ten years old that my family's super size would become something of a national phenomenon. That was the year a cable network, TLC, featured a documentary on our family, back when there were *just* fourteen kids. While I didn't know any life different from the one I had, people outside of our big family community and lifestyle were fascinated by the number of kids and how life worked for a bigger-than-average household. It's a paradox I still find myself sorting out today, that while I thought my life was utterly normal, even with all the siblings around me and television cameras always in my face, there was an audience who saw my life as anything *but* normal. For the next seventeen years, my family, my upbringing, my life would be featured on television through specials, two different series, interviews, and all kinds of other broadcasts.

There's a saying that fish can't see water, meaning that when you're in the middle of something, when it's your whole world, when it's what you breathe and swim in, you can't see things for what they really are. I'd say, in many ways, that saying captures what much of my life was like. I didn't know what I didn't know. In one of my previous books, *Becoming Free Indeed*, I laid out the experience of growing up not just in a big family but in a religious system known as the Institute in Basic Life Principles (IBLP). It was controlling, male-centered, and legalistic, under the ironclad grip of a leader named Bill Gothard. It was important to me in that book to point out the specific theological errors of that system, to help equip others to understand and find freedom from cultlike organizations that undermine the power and beauty of how Jesus teaches us to live.

Whether you've already read that book or we're meeting here for the first time on the printed page, I wanted you to have this background as context: that religious system and its requirements were at the core of how I saw myself and how I judged myself. The echo of that system's demands would ricochet off the fragile edges of my soul for years, inflicting damage that, at some level, I could feel but couldn't see until I experienced the healing medicine of gospel grace.

Where did that change begin?

Enter Jeremy Vuolo.

I told a friend recently that of all the big personalities in my life, my husband, Jeremy, is the biggest and my favorite. He has a way of drawing a crowd with his wit and his humor. He's the life of the party, the guide on our adventures, the person who knows how to have fun. He's joy personified. He grew up on the other side of the country from me, he traveled the world as a professional soccer player, and he is regularly the guy behind the mic talking about his faith. We met when he came to visit my sister Jessa and her husband, Ben, at a Gothard conference. Jeremy wasn't part of the Gothard group, and it showed. It was obvious that he loved God, that he cared deeply about people, *and* that he wasn't afraid to laugh, to have a different opinion, and to ask hard questions. It was like all the windows were thrown open when Jeremy entered the room, airing out the stuffiness and letting the fresh breeze in.

It was also kind of terrifying.

He was so handsome and so fun and so . . . alive. Because I was so steeped in the IBLP way of looking at things, I thought it was a potential step into sin to even acknowledge that I was attracted to Jeremy, that I felt my heart tugged in his direction. I didn't say a word about him to my sister Jessa at that first meeting—not a giggle, not a blush.

But here's the thing about Jeremy. He's going to shoot his shot, whether on the soccer field, in the pulpit, or in any other area of his life. He did that for me. Because of the religious system I was part of, he had to run an unfamiliar obstacle course of permissions, conversations, and even a fifty-page questionnaire to begin the process of pursuing me. When we were both on a mission trip to Honduras and El Salvador, just a few months after meeting, my nerves were all over the place. And once we fell in love, the vibrancy of Jeremy's outlook, faith, and devotion began to crack open a wider world of mercy and grace to me. As our love story grew, I found myself seeing something unexpected, that there was light and lightness on the other side of the door of shame and condemnation. Jeremy didn't just show me that; he lived it.

We got married in 2016, and today, we have two daughters, Felicity and Evangeline. We live in Los Angeles, California, where we work, serve our church, spend sunny days outside with the kids, splurge on our favorite coffees, and continue to build a story for our family with Jesus Christ as the cornerstone. And it's where my healing continues.

If you've known nothing of my story before now or if you watched every episode of my time on television, I want to make sure, as we start this journey together, that you have my perspective on my past and on my present. Not what a videographer or editor on television thought you should see. Not what a magazine says. Not what a rumor claims or a paparazzi shot shows. I want you to hear it from me.

From the downfall of Bill Gothard to the horrible revelations about one of my siblings, here's one of the most important things I've learned: I won't live a lie. I've seen what happens when we pretend to be one thing, when we perform and posture while our reality is something else. And I've seen what happens when you and I are honest about our challenges, our struggles, our fears, and our mistakes. The light gets in. The grace shows up. Freedom is the experience of truth.

Old friend, new friend, however we've found each other, here we are today. Thank you for being here. It's my prayer that in sharing another chapter of my story, you find help, healing, and freedom in your own.

Chapter 1

CONFESSION: I'M A PEOPLE PLEASER

THE APARTMENT WAS CLEAN AND COZY. THE DINNER was prepped and in the oven, the yummy scent of melting cheese and butter in the air. I'd added a couple of cute decor items to our coffee table and shelf unit that I'd found on one of my thrifting hunts, and they looked great. Our dining table, which was a normal-sized table but seemed huge in our compact apartment, was spread with our collection of plates and napkins and utensils.

Jeremy and I were just a few months into our brand-new marriage, living in Laredo, Texas, in an apartment a mile or two from the border. I'd moved down to Texas after our wedding as Jeremy continued his work as a pastor at a local church.

From the get-go of our relationship, Jeremy and I connected in so many ways. One of the things we both held in high importance was that we wanted to create a home that was for hosting. We both love to entertain, and we both love time spent with friends. When we were engaged and dreaming of the future, we talked about having people over for meals and game nights and small groups. We were ready to build and cultivate relationships in our new married life together. We agreed to make hosting people a strategic part of our household budget, both financially and with our time. We'd talk about what food we could prepare and who we could invite and how much fun it would all be.

And we made good on all those plans. Just a few months into our marriage, we were routinely having people over, sharing food and laughter and stories, just like we talked about when we were getting to know each other. It was all the things I'd hoped for, building a life and ministry with Jeremy, gathering awesome people around us, giving those who were feeling lonely a place to belong. I'd furnished our apartment with these goals in mind. I was spending a good chunk of my time doing all the things that need to be done when you're having people over, wanting to make sure our guests were comfortable and able to gather in a pretty, cozy, clean space.

I had a great husband, was beginning some sweet friendships, and was getting to do all the things I'd said I'd wanted. From the outside, it all looked good.

So why was I consumed with this feeling, this dark cloud of *dread*?

Why, even with everything ready to go, the chores done, and the doorbell about to start ringing, did I feel this way every time? Every. Time.

Why?

———

How cool would it be if there was a Control+F (Command-F if you're Mac-fancy) function in life? Hear me out. If you could somehow look back over your life, hit Control+F, and "find" all the places where certain issues, patterns, and words come up, imagine how much faster that could make the process of figuring out why you do the things you do, why you say the things you say, you feel the way you feel.

I got to have a Control+F experience, literally, while working on my last book, *Becoming Free Indeed*. It revealed something that was right there the whole time, but I saw it with greater frequency and importance than I'd ever realized before. If you were to go into a digital copy of that book, which is about my journey of breaking free from the harmful beliefs and influence of the religious system I was raised in, and you were to Control+F the words *people pleaser*, your screen would light up like a Christmas tree. Even though people pleasing wasn't what that book was about, there was no denying that because of the way I'm wired and the environment of the culture around me, people pleasing has had a grip on me for a long time.

It makes sense now, but I have to tell you that it took me kind of by surprise, realizing that people pleasing was a phantom heartbeat in my life. Someone recently asked me when I became truly aware that I was dealing with being a people pleaser. After all, from the way I was raised to how I naturally came wired, trying to keep everybody happy and on an even keel was simply part of my original operating system. A few years ago, even back to those days as a newlywed in Laredo, I don't think I could have seen that people pleasing was at the core of everything I was dealing with.

I thought I was a nervous hostess. I thought I was an anxious student during my homeschool days. I thought I was a perfectionist about my housekeeping. I thought I was sincere and simply careful (and scared) in the way I was trying to keep every command I was told God had given me.

I didn't know why managing my emotions, my stress, and my jitters felt so hard. I was doing everything I knew in order to avoid any kind of confrontation or failure. I was doing everything I knew in order to be the most "perfect" I could be. I also knew that I was miserable.

What I didn't know was why.

———

Which brings me back to that day at my newlywed apartment, getting ready to host new friends from our church. My mind would simply not stop whirling. My body was tense, and my stomach was in knots. I'd love to tell you that everything worked out just fine, that our guests came over, and I realized that everyone was comfortable and happy and that the next time we had people over, I didn't go through the same cyclone of terror and dismay.

But . . . that's not what happened.

The feelings just got bigger, and the darkness got darker. There were times I felt like I was standing outside of myself, watching this girl I barely recognized fall apart at the smallest notion of letting people down.

How had I gotten here?

I retreated more and more from the community we'd been so excited to build. But the feelings just kept growing. I would have to wrestle with intense anxiety while I was getting ready for church, already filled with apprehension at who I might have to talk to, what would happen if I said something stupid, how it might reflect on Jeremy. I turned down invitations to go to coffee. I kept trying to make my world smaller and smaller in an effort to make my panic smaller.

Spoiler: it didn't work.

When you're a people pleaser, all your thrashing to make your feelings smaller, all your *managing*, ultimately drags you down deeper into the waters of big trouble.

———

When I use the phrase *people pleaser,* I know what I mean by it, but I want to make sure you and I are on the same page. As it turns out, a lot of different feelings come with pleasing people. In my early days in Laredo, people pleasing felt like dread and anxiety. But I can also remember other times it felt like sadness or nerves. And I remember still other times I felt really proud that I had accomplished or said or done something in the way that another person wanted me to. I loved it when people praised me for my compliance to their wishes.

People pleasing *feels* a lot of different ways.

But people pleasing at its core is this: when we put everyone else's preferences and opinions above our own or above what we know is true and right for the purpose of gaining acceptance and approval or to avoid criticism. It's when we feel like someone else's approval is critical to our survival and our understanding of our worth. It's when we lose the ability to stand up for ourselves in order to keep someone else happy. It's when we'd rather just go along than have that tough conversation or confront harmful behavior in someone else.

In a nutshell, people pleasing is when someone else's approval, happiness, preference, or opinion comes before anything else in your world. And your whole world is built around accommodating those things for them in order to gain their approval, whether they've directly told you that's what they expect or you've imagined it all on your own.

If you're someone who was raised in church, you might think, *Now wait a minute, Jinger. I thought God wanted us to put other people before ourselves.* And you're not wrong; Scripture does talk about not thinking more highly of ourselves than we should (Romans 12:3). Jesus does teach about going the extra mile for others (Matthew 5:41).

But here's the difference. It's all about motive—what you're trying to get by people pleasing. Are you walking in humility? Are you walking in generosity for the right reasons? Or are you appeasing

But people pleasing at its core is this: when we put everyone else's preferences and opinions above our own or above what we know is true and right for the purpose of gaining acceptance and approval or to avoid criticism.

people around you because you want their approval and acceptance? Seeking acceptance or seeking to avoid disapproval are the two big mile markers on the people-pleasing path. And both of those will get you twisted in knots eventually.

While some verses talk about serving others well and caring for them, there are plenty of other places in Scripture that talk about *not* trying to please others. Proverbs 29:25 says, "The fear of man lays a snare, but whoever trusts in the LORD is safe." It's that word *snare* that really stands out to me. My people pleasing has always been about me trying not to get "snared" or "trapped" by someone's upset or anger or disappointment. But in turning myself inside out in that effort, I was trapped in my own skin, mute to speak what I really thought or needed, caught between bars of the expectations of others and the ones I'd put on myself.

I also entered the trap of seeking approval. My understanding of my own worth was so wrapped up in someone telling me I was doing a good job or that I was so easy to be around. And when all you know of yourself is what someone else is telling you about yourself, it's a cage like no other.

What has people pleasing cost you? Have you let yourself down, making a choice you wouldn't have otherwise, were it not for the pressure you felt from others? I have. Have you put up with someone treating you in a way you wouldn't let them get away with toward a friend? Maybe you have let the idea of possibly letting someone down consume you so much that you haven't gone for a particular opportunity. Maybe you feel a pulse of people pleasing course through you when you know you should say something . . . but you don't.

Feel like I'm reading your journal? It's because I've been there, and on bad days, I still go there a little bit, the muscle memory of people pleasing leading me down some of the same familiar paths and feelings.

But I've got good news for us. I'm learning that it is possible to get free from the web of it. It's not easy. It takes staring down yourself and your motives and your behaviors with an honest eye. It requires honesty and courage and failing and trying again. It means you'll have to let go of some patterns, definitions, and relationships that are keeping you tangled up.

And you don't have to do it alone.

———

There's something about a fresh start that can help you see things from a new perspective. For me, that was the move we made from Laredo to Los Angeles in 2019. As we emptied out our first little apartment and packed boxes of our belongings, it was like a camera lens zoomed out for me. I was not only packing up my house but also putting a bunch of hard and harmful emotions in the box to take with me as well. I was already practicing the awkward and nervous encounters that come with needing to make new friends. I was already anticipating the darkness I would feel, the panic of having new people over, the worry about how I would be perceived, the dread. *Will these new people in my new town in my new chapter of life like me . . . or think I am stuck up . . . or reject me . . . or judge me?* It was like I was carefully packaging up the dark feelings I'd had in Laredo with bubble wrap, nestling them alongside the wedding china, ready to take them out in my new city and unwrap all that difficulty to be put on the shelf as damaging decor. It was like I could see myself from above, packing up those feelings, getting ready to be a hot mess all over again.

That's not healthy, I thought. *It's not good.*

I wouldn't necessarily say it was a lightbulb moment, but it was one of the first times that, instead of letting the feelings drive me, I considered the cost of those feelings. For me, something shifted. I didn't want to repeat the patterns of my Laredo experience. When we hit the ground in our new city of Los Angeles, rather than pulling out the scary yet familiar reactions and thoughts I'd experienced before, I slowly began simply taking note of when those feelings would start to bubble rather than letting them run.

It took a lot of time. It took a lot of counsel. It took a lot of prayer. It took a lot of talking to Jeremy about what I was experiencing in my head. It took a lot of believing Jeremy that he loved me regardless.

And over time, little by little, I made friends and had people over without as many tears, and I made small steps of progress.

Honestly, through that process, I don't know that I would have told you that at the core of all of those feelings and reactions was a deep-seated issue of people pleasing. I got to know the feelings and the triggers well and was intentional in getting the help I needed to get it all untangled. But at that point, I still wasn't clear what was at the core. In the midst of it, I began work on *Becoming Free Indeed*.

I thought I was getting ahead of some of those unhealthy emotions, but the book-writing process got me all cranked up again. I couldn't stop thinking about what people would think of me as I was truthfully exposing facets of the harmful theology I'd been raised in. I didn't want to hurt anyone who was still involved in overbearing and legalistic religious systems. *What are they going to think?* I worried. *What if they reject me? What if they see me as some kind of traitor?* But this time, I had better tools to figure some things out. And I also had an even bigger sense of mission than my emotions could mute.

See, I believe that in the writing of that book, I had an absolute responsibility to call out the teaching I had been raised in and to do my part to help others become free from those kinds of systems. I believe I have a God-given charge to do what I can to shine light into the dark places of harmful religious systems. That sense of assignment, and that love for others who are trapped in some of the same thinking and fear that I was, is more powerful than the dark emotions that have left me spinning for approval.

So there it was. With better tools available to me, and with a clarity of charge, I kept writing, even through worry and fear. And then, as the words flowed and the stories were told, that term just kept cropping up: *people pleasing*.

There it was, right on the page. All those feelings that had haunted me for so long were moths to the flame around that phrase. What had seemed murky was now highlighted in neon. I was a people pleaser. Like I said, you could Control+F and see it plain as day.

It was clear: for me, a big part of freedom is becoming free from people pleasing. Because I'm so passionate about helping you become free from things that hold you back, and because I want to live in the freedom Jesus came to give me, it became very obvious and very important to me to tackle this topic.

But to be honest, I'm already a little worried.

Worried about what you'll think of me. Worried you won't find me relatable. Worried that if I talk about certain experiences I've had in my life, you might think I'm showing off or acting like I've got it all figured out. Worried that if there are things I don't talk about, you'll think I'm hiding. Worried that you might think I'm trying to come off as some kind of expert when I know how far I have to go.

Worried you won't like me.

Hi. I'm Jinger with a *J*. And I'm recovering from an epic case of being a big people pleaser. As in a chronic one. There's nothing like launching a project like a book on people pleasing to make you discover new places you'll need to overcome. I've come a long way, but, my friend, I've got a long way to go.

From the earliest age I can remember, I was a follower. I followed my sister Jessa everywhere. I followed all the rules. I followed the "spiritual" strong opinions around me.

For most of my life, I followed the rules to a T. Chores done on time, Sunday school lessons followed like an unbreakable to-do list, homework in by deadline—those were all the major priorities of my life. I wanted my parents to be happy. I wanted my friends to like me. The idea of having an argument or being on someone's bad side made me feel a heavy weight in my chest. It would hang over me all day like a dark cloud. And, just like you, I'd bet, all those people-pleasing tendencies earned me lots of kudos from people around me. Let's face it: when you're a chronic people pleaser, it's pretty convenient for the people around you. You, like me, have probably gotten plenty of "atta girls" for being so "dependable" and "responsible" and "easygoing."

But the internal price you and I have paid for bringing so much convenience to everyone else? It's a big one.

I've learned that it's the motives behind those traits that become the problem. And even though I'd worked so hard to always keep the waters calm and people happy, there's only so much pleasing you can do until it all catches up with you.

It looked cool and refreshing. Inviting. Soothing.

But . . .

I can't, I'd think.

And I wasn't wrong.

I truly couldn't.

When I'd stand at the edge of a pool or on the beach before a wave, I knew the water would drag me down, pull the air from my lungs, toss me in the tide.

I couldn't swim.

I wanted to. Since I was a little girl, I had wanted to know what it felt like to push myself through the water, to swing my arms and kick my legs to keep me at the surface. But I didn't know how.

Here's what I did know for sure: long skirts were not designed for learning how to swim. Yep, we're already talking about long skirts. Regardless of how you might have arrived at a fashion place of wearing them, I'm here to tell you that the laws of physics, gravity, and buoyancy don't play well with long skirts.

How do I know this? Because I tried swimming in them when I was younger, and it went about as well as you'd think.

Another way of saying "long-skirt swimmer" is "one who sinks."

And because long skirts were the only swimming fashion available to me as a kid, and because I had a thing about not wanting to sink, the skill of swimming was not something I picked up during that time.

When you don't know how to swim, water of all kinds gets scary. On a boat, in a kayak, at a pool, all of it makes you feel in over your head—pun unintended.

Fast-forward to Los Angeles, living that Southern California coastal life, along with some of the high temperatures we get around here, and you're surrounded by the beach, swimming pools, water parks, lakes, and rivers. Add to that the fact that I'm raising children in this outdoor water world. I want them to know how to swim. I want them to know that I can too.

But I was still so scared, thinking back to the few times I'd tried as a kid, the long skirt encasing my flailing legs. My earlier attempts at swimming only brought back those feelings, desperately thrashing to keep my nose above the water line. And for some reason, I was really hesitant to try again, because I was embarrassed that I didn't already know how. And I was scared to fail.

It was my friend Rebekah who led the way. "I'll show you," she assured me. "We'll take it slow." She offered to let me come learn in her pool, where I could try and fail and try again in the privacy of her backyard. She showed me some things while still on dry land—how to move my arms, how to think about where my body would be in the water. She encouraged me and used herself as an example and let me take it slow.

We're still at it, my swimming lessons, taking it baby step by baby step (or maybe I should say baby lap by baby lap).

It has required having the right equipment for the job.

It has required being willing to be scared.

It has required getting help.

It has required being humble enough to accept that help.

It has required being uncomfortable in order to learn how to be comfortable in the water.

And, yes, it has required me to ditch the long denim skirt.

As we dive into these waters together, I hope to be for you what my friend Rebekah has been for me. Rebekah is no Olympian in the water and makes no claim to be. But she knows the water, knows things that don't work, understands the fear, and knows how to keep herself afloat. And she's willing to share her experiences and what she knows to do with me.

I've tried swimming in the waters of life, trying to stay afloat when my people-pleasing tendencies were dragging me down. I can't promise you that I'm ready to sign up for a triathlon next week (but I'm working on it!), but what I can promise you is that I know the feelings you're experiencing in your people pleasing and I've learned some things that can help. Things that can help us float and paddle and get further upstream.

Maybe you're just toe-dipping with the idea of changing some of your people-pleasing ways. Maybe you're floundering in the shallow end, trying to figure out how to get the courage to paddle out into deeper waters. Or maybe you feel like you're drowning in the expectations of others and yourself. Maybe you're soaked through with the voice in your head that critiques all the things you're doing wrong, cites all the things you need to change, on repeat 24/7.

I've been there. At first, my people pleasing was how I kept my fear of who I really was and what I really wanted at bay. Then there were those years when I could feel a deepening sense of panic that I was starting to get trapped in all the folds of what everyone was putting on me. There was that sense of drowning in my early marriage, as the depths of all the pleasing I'd been carrying began to drag me further and further down.

Now?

By God's grace, I've broken through the surface. I'm learning who I am and how to speak up for myself. I'm discovering what God has intended for me, and what He never meant for me to be captive to.

When I started the writing process of this book, I felt unqualified to be your guide. Frankly, I still do. As I say, I've still got a long way to go. I know this is a skirmish that will probably always be fought at the borders of my heart. But what I can do is go first and tell you my story.

My heartbeat for you and for myself is to live in the freedom that Jesus came to give us. I want you to be free from the bondage of living in fear—the fear of rejection, imperfection, and criticism. And I want you to be set free to love people well for the right reasons, without thought of return. Free to discover how God created you to enjoy Him and thrive in healthy community. Free to live for God's approval instead of everyone else's.

I just want you to be free.

Let's Chat About It

At the conclusion of each chapter of this book, you'll find some questions to consider, a verse or a prayer to think on, and some encouragement as you move through this journey. I love books that have this kind of wrap-up at the end of chapters, which is why I wanted to do this for you. It's an opportunity for you and me to "chat" through the pages about what really caught our attention, where we have a deeper understanding of how we've been struggling, and where we can see we're growing. So think back on what you've just read.

1. Why did you pick up this book? What about the idea of people pleasing caught your attention?
2. What do you hope to learn about people pleasing and about yourself as we walk through the following chapters together?

Chapter 2

NEW TOOLS

I TRY TO BE ORGANIZED. I REALLY DO.

But with small kids and a busy schedule and stuff flying at me all the time, sometimes the wheels come off.

Take, for example, a morning when I'm trying to get out the door on time and my keys have gone missing. It's happened to you, right? Keys that you know you had the day before that have now disappeared. Yes, I know that putting my keys in the same place every time I come in the door is the solution. And for the most part, I pull it off. But sometimes I'm carrying in one of the kids, and I've got a diaper bag over one shoulder and grocery bags strung like gourds on a vine on the other. (Please tell me you do this too, that Olympic sport known as Trying to Carry as Many Kids and Bags in from the Car in the Fewest Trips.)

I finally make it in the door with all the kids, backpacks, books, groceries, and all the rest, and before I can even start getting things where they belong, there's a phone call or a child who needs a drink of water or some other event that diverts my attention.

All of which leads to the next morning, when I start searching for my keys and they are nowhere to be found.

The wildest thing to me about the lost key search is, once I find them—after a lot of frustration and turning everything upside down—how obvious it is where they are. *Of course they were on that bookcase, because I came in the door, and then my daughter tripped, and I set the keys there to pick her up . . .*

Well, obvious after the fact.

That's how people pleasing was in my life, like I was telling you earlier. It was right in front of me, but I was so busy spinning on all the things that it became just part of the scenery.

Now, I have to think that if you've picked up a book on people pleasing, you have a pretty good idea that you might be dealing with some people-pleasing issues in your life. That means you're already further down the road than I was when I started to get clear about what was holding me back in my relationships, inner life, and fears.

Wherever you are, I want to help us both gain even more clarity about how much people pleasing affects us day-to-day. I believe we can't start making changes and making gains until we have a good picture of how much something is affecting us. For example, I thought my people pleasing was keeping me safe . . . until I realized it was putting me in danger of isolation. If we are willing to stare down just how much of a people pleaser we are and where it is limiting our joy, our relationships, our trust, and the whole of our lives, we can start to move past our negative people-pleasing ways.

My oldest sister, Jana, recently came for a visit, and it was awesome. We put in the time for some required sightseeing, sipped on lots of lattes, and laughed and reminisced.

My favorite part?

We built stuff.

I haven't thought of myself as a DIY kind of a person until now, but Jana is the undisputed DIY queen. The girl builds stuff. All kinds of stuff. If she sees something she wants to build, she'll do it. It could be an arbor in a garden, a bookshelf, a chicken coop, or a table. Literally anything she sets her mind to.

I was really excited for Jana to see my new house and took her on a tour of the family room, the kitchen, the bedrooms. I told her about the various plans we had for each of the spaces, and while we were in the guest bedroom, I explained to her what I wanted to do in the closet to make it more functional and aesthetic.

"We can build that," she told me.

Huh?

We, as in, Jana and me?

Sure enough, with images of possible closet customization dancing in my head before all of my "I can'ts!" came rushing in, Jana hustled me off to the hardware store, snapping out a tape measure, making notes on her phone, sketching out a plan, and gathering supplies. You should see her in the home improvement store; she's in her element. We stacked wood and supplies on a lumber cart, Jana casually steering the thing to the front of the store, coffee cup in one hand, pulling the wonky cart with the other, cool as a cucumber.

Before I knew it, we were back in my closet, ripping out the old shelves and rods and diving in, Jana's quiet confidence in the project lighting the way.

Watching Jana work on a project like this and getting to serve as her novice but eager assistant was a thing of beauty. This smart, beautiful sister of mine truly has a special touch when it comes to creating order and beauty with tools and a paintbrush. It's like some incredible second language she speaks, with her understanding of how things should be laid out, how to make it secure and efficient and beautiful. And it's a language she had the patience to start teaching me. Through the whole process, she explained what she was doing and why, showed me how to use a variety of tools and techniques, and set the standard for what we wanted to accomplish so the final product would be what I wanted.

After a few hours of putting it all together, we stood back to admire our work, the scent of fresh-cut lumber in the air (which should be its own candle scent, BTW). I was pretty giddy.

There was a new space for hanging clothes. A shelved alcove for extra linens and pillows. And then there was my very favorite part: long lines of shelves for my beloved shoes. I quickly started lining the shelves with my sneakers, heels, and boots, sorting everything by color and style. Maybe it's not your kind of Instagram-worthy setup, but let me tell you, I felt like some kind of home decor influencer snapping pics of what we had created.

In one day, Jana took me from feeling like there was no way I could build something like this to having a better understanding of what it takes and how to do it.

Before Jana came to visit, before I ever dreamed we could rip out one closet and custom-build another, a friend had given us a circular saw. It had been sitting in the garage, and I had no idea how to use it or what all I could use it for, other than getting in a workout as I moved it from one side of the garage to the other, trying to figure out where I should store it. But when Jana came to town, and we decided to put on our DIY crowns for the day, she showed me how to use the circular saw. To say that it sped up our building process would be an understatement; I can only imagine how long it would have taken to cut the lumber by hand for a project that required lots and lots and lots of measuring and cutting. I'd probably still have a ripped-out, empty shell of a closet to this day!

When you see how much more efficiently you can move forward when you've got the right equipment, that's the kind of lesson that stays with you. It's made me think about the variety of things I've tried to tackle in the past when I didn't have the right tool. No wonder I would get frustrated and feel like I couldn't do it, like I wasn't capable!

For this reason, you might want to go find your favorite pen and highlighter and spend the next little while working through an assessment I've put together for you. It's a simple tool that I believe will help you understand more about where you are as a people pleaser and some of the things that may have gotten you here. I don't mean for this assessment to be some scientific, super-official sort of a thing; we both know I'm not claiming to be any kind of self-help guru.

I'm someone just like you, who wants to come alongside you as you're taking steps toward your own freedom. These are the questions I'm asking myself in my own people-pleasing journey, finding greater clarity and identifying some patterns so I, with God's help, can find the off-ramp. It's the chance to pause, slow down, and really observe what's driving you and your motives for your behaviors with other people.

Take your time with this. You might want to answer everything all in one sitting, or you may find that you need to take a breather and think about a question before answering. If you find yourself writing long responses, great. And if you find that you can answer in just a few words, that's fine too. It's not about trying to write an award-winning essay or anything. I just want you to put words—your own thoughtful, meaningful words—to the presence and impact of unhealthy people pleasing in your life.

Take your time. Be honest. I'm going to say that again: be honest. Don't write down what you think someone else would want to hear. Don't answer in a way that you think might sound more "spiritual." You will likely feel a tug to perform for others with these questions because that's what we typically do, you and I, responding first with what we think others want us to do and say.

Look: these pages, these questions? They're for you and you alone. You don't have to share. It's just you and the page and as much honesty as you can muster.

So get to it, friend, and I'll be waiting for you on the other side. As Proverbs 20:5 says, "The purpose in a man's heart is like deep water, but a man of understanding will draw it out."

People Pleaser Assessment

- Why did you pick up this book? What about the title made you think that it was something you should read?
- Have you ever used the words *people pleaser* to describe yourself? Why or why not?
- Have others ever used the words *people pleaser* to describe you? What was one of the situations in which someone referred to you as a people pleaser? (Note: sometimes someone might not use the term *people pleaser* but say something like, "You're such a chameleon" or "You're always worried about what people think.")
- Write down a few other words to describe yourself—any that come to mind.
- Sometimes we use words that sound positive to describe people-pleasing ways. Are any of the following words sometimes how people describe you?

    Helpful
    Compliant
    Easygoing
    Considerate
    Laid-back
    Cooperative
    Peacemaker
    Caregiver
    Accommodating
    Self-sacrificing
    Generous

- If you have been described as any of those terms, what were the conditions in which you were called that?
- How did you feel following any of those interactions? Did you feel fulfilled or energized? Burned-out or resentful? Flat? Excited? Take your time to really think back about it.
- How would you describe your most consistent current emotional state?
- On a scale of one to ten, with one being "rarely or never" and ten being "almost all the time," where would you rate yourself on how often you think about what other people might be thinking?
- The kinds of environments we were raised in, what we got praise for, what we got in trouble for—those things all impact our tendencies toward people pleasing, and I'm not just talking about faith backgrounds here. What kind of environment would you say you were raised in? What did you get kudos for?
- Sometimes, when others are trying to shape or control our behavior, they do it by one of three approaches: *submission*, in which you feel forced to behave or act a certain way because of the consequences if you don't; *manipulation*, in which you are guilt-tripped or deceived; or *flattery*, in which you are overly complimented and praised, all for the purpose of getting the other person what they want from you. Do you feel others have tried to use these approaches to control you? If so, has it worked? Why do you think that is?
- How do you think the combination of your environment and the style of control you've experienced from others has affected your choices and decisions today?
- As you think back to your childhood and your teenage years, who was the person who was most influential in your life? What made them so influential to you?
- What are some of the things you remember them saying about life and about you?

- What does it feel like when someone shows you their approval?
- What does it feel like in your body when someone seems displeased with you?
- On a scale of one to ten, with one meaning "meh" and ten meaning "it means everything to me," what does receiving approval feel like to you?
- What is the craziest, silliest, or hardest thing you've done in the name of seeking someone's approval?
- Write down a time you attended an event, took on a project, or volunteered for something that you weren't sure you wanted to be a part of. Thinking back to that thing, what are the feelings you remember about taking that on?
  - Were you scared to tell someone no?
  - Did you feel pressured?
  - Did you feel guilty about not being involved, and so you signed up?
  - Write down as many of the feelings you can remember.
- Before I got married, I went through a season in which I now look back on and think of myself as being "extra" in how I presented myself spiritually. I read through the entire Bible in just a handful of weeks. If friends were over for a movie night, I would excuse myself and go upstairs to pray while they all enjoyed the movie. I stopped laughing as much. I forced myself to become a quieter, much more reserved version of myself, to the point that one of my friends said to me, "Jinger, you're so quiet. I just sometimes wonder what's going on inside your head." I went from having an outgoing, bubbly personality to being this super pious, serious, withdrawn person. And why? Because for some reason, I thought forcing myself into that character would get me more of God's approval.
  - If you're a follower of Jesus, how are you seeking God's approval?

- If you're not yet a believer, what have you heard about God and His acceptance of you? Has it sounded to you like you can earn His approval through good deeds? Do you pop into a church service for, say, Easter or Christmas, thinking that will earn you some points? Why?

You did it! I'm proud of you. It takes a special kind of courage to face your memories and motivations. There will be times throughout the book when I ask you to pop back over here and take a look at what you've written on specific questions, to help you connect the dots on how people pleasing shows up in your life. We all have a unique people-pleasing profile within a familiar pattern. When we are more aware of how we veer into our people-pleasing ways and why, it can make it all the faster to cut off what doesn't serve us, just like Jana and I killing it with that circular saw.

There's something else I want you to notice about your own style of people pleasing. To me, there are two kinds of motives in people pleasing. One is the motive of seeking approval. You don't feel so great about yourself, so you're looking for others' approval to make you feel okay. This is the kind of people pleasing I see in this verse: "They loved the glory that comes from man more than the glory that comes from God" (John 12:43).

The other motive is to try to avoid doing anything to upset someone or warrant their criticism. It's like when God told Moses to go confront Pharoah, the Egyptian ruler who was keeping the Hebrew people in slavery. Moses was so afraid of what he considered to be his lack of speaking skills that he said to God, "Oh, my Lord, please send someone else" (Exodus 4:13).

I tend to be the wallflower Moses kind of people pleaser; if I'm afraid I'm going to disappoint you, I'll just fade into the background and shut down. I know other people pleasers who go the opposite direction; they'll just keep trying harder and keep going bigger and keep pursuing others' approval, no matter the cost. I think of them as the disco people pleasers, getting bigger and flashier to offset rejection. And yes, there are people who fall somewhere in between, but I think a lot of us tend to go one way or the other. Where do you think you tend to go? Write it down.

As you worked your way through the questions, what did you start to notice? A couple of things really pop up for me. I tend to jump into any kind of work behind the scenes, wanting to take the burden off others, which, in and of itself, can be a great way to serve. But as I stare down my motives, I find I still want to make sure no one has anything bad to say about me, and I use service as a way to try to pay some kind of ransom against any kind of negative opinion debt about me.

So what is it for you?

———

We all struggle for different and nuanced reasons. But I do think, at its core, we're all fighting for the same things—things we think we might get by people pleasing:

1. to feel like we have a place we belong, and
2. to avoid being excluded, misunderstood, and criticized.

I recently heard something that got me thinking. I heard someone talking about how being included as part of a group was, for a very long time, an important part of survival in the human experience. If you were living in a tiny farming village in the wilds of, say, Ireland, and you managed to get your handful of farming village buddies mad at you—mad to the point where they cut you off—your very life was at risk. If you didn't keep friendly connections with those around you, you could find yourself not just out of a community but possibly even at battle with them. If you ran out of water or food, the members of your community would be the ones you would turn to. If you got sick, those were the people who would help care for you. And if you had upset them in the past, if you had displeased them, then you could have been signing your own death sentence when you had a significant need come along and they were no longer willing to help you.

I'd never really thought about people pleasing as a survival skill. We're going to unpack more about this later, but for now, as you think about all the things you wrote down in the earlier assessment, as you take a fresh look at where you are, I want to encourage you in this: you're a survivor.

It's likely why you've been trying to please others all these years. Maybe it was to keep you safe from someone's anger and abuse. Maybe it was to hang on to the job you desperately needed to support you and your baby. Maybe it was an attempt to find your place socially at school or church. Maybe it was to try to manage the volatile emotions of an extended family member.

My point is, I don't think you and I have been people pleasing just to try to be the most popular kid on the block. We learned somewhere along the way that during hard and unpredictable and scary times, the one thing we could try to do was make everybody happy. Because if we could make everybody happy, maybe, just maybe, we could keep bad things from happening.

——————

Jeremy and I drove through a beautiful part of the East Coast with a friend, an area in New Jersey just outside of New York City. All kinds of celebrities and financially successful people make their home there, and elaborate custom houses are under construction everywhere you look. What we found particularly fascinating was that the first things being built into the heart of these homes, once the foundation had been laid, were panic rooms. Panic rooms are built with specific safety features, often deep in the heart of a house. Why would these successful people make a panic room the most consistent feature we saw in all this custom building, regardless of the style of each house?

As humans, we were designed to need love, joy, and peace. Those are actually the first three fruits of the Spirit listed by Paul in his letter to the people living in Galatia (Galatians 5:22–23). We want love because we were built for relationships. We want joy because we were designed to be happy, and we want peace, which is a drive for safety. That's what those panic rooms represented—a way to try to create a sense of peace, that drive for safety. No matter your resources, your level of fame, whatever, we all want to have some sense of security. For you and me, people pleasing has likely been our form of a panic room, a command center from which we operate our relationships because we so badly don't want to get hurt, don't want to be exposed. We can think it's a way to get to love and joy, even though a panic room is a dead end.

I wonder if this is part of why Jesus showed so much compassion to people. I think He knew and understood that, for a lot of us, we're just trying to get by. It doesn't mean He would want us to stay stuck—not at all. Jesus spent a chunk of His ministry here on earth helping people get free from the things that were holding them back.

One day, Jesus came to a town as He was traveling. Two thousand years ago, during the time Jesus was here on earth, the central hub for a lot of towns was the town well. It's where you would go to get your drinking water and the water needed for your household duties. It was a place to gather as a community, to catch up on the latest gossip, to swap recipes and remedies, kind of like when we run into neighbors in the bread aisle at the local grocery store today. So when Jesus was going through the town of Sychar, He stopped at the local well.

While He was at the well, He met a local woman, a Samaritan. That means she came from a line of people with a history of being

Jewish, but some of the beliefs and practices of her people veered away from traditional Judaism. In biblical times, that put the Jews and Samaritans at odds with each other. For Jesus to talk with her, both a woman and a Samaritan, shows Jesus' character; He's not all that interested in what society has to say about you. He's interested in who *you* are, just as you are.

As Jesus and the Samaritan woman talked, Jesus was direct and honest with her. She'd had a string of bad marriages and was currently in yet another relationship that wasn't honoring to herself or to God. Jesus didn't shy away from talking about the truth of her situation. He talked about her history, her choices. They had themselves a little assessment tool moment, right there at the town well, in the heat of the day.

Jesus wasn't scolding her or accusatory. He was just talking about the facts with her. He was giving her a new way of thinking about where her life had been, where it was going on its current path, and what it could be, if she chose to go a different way. And in the days that followed, more of the townspeople talked with Jesus. The Bible says in John 4:39–42:

> Many Samaritans from that town believed in him because of the woman's testimony, "He told me all that I ever did." So when the Samaritans came to him, they asked him to stay with them, and he stayed there two days. And many more believed because of his word. They said to the woman, "It is no longer because of what you said that we believe, for we have heard for ourselves, and we know that this is indeed the Savior of the world."

That's what truth can do when we face the truth about ourselves with the help of Jesus. We are freed from the patterns that have dictated our behaviors. And we can help others find freedom as well.

We've come to this moment recognizing that our people pleasing, if continued, will only bring us a muted life and a muted voice.

Your people pleasing holds many of the seeds for what is best and delightful about you; you've just been sowing a lot of the gifts into the wrong ground and for the wrong reasons.

I don't want that for you, and I don't want that for myself. But let's take a beat to acknowledge that you and I are people pleasers because we saw it as a way to solve a problem that seemed overwhelming. We have been willing to give up so much of ourselves, but why? What are the things that drive us in this way? Your people pleasing holds many of the seeds for what is best and delightful about you; you've just been sowing a lot of the gifts into the wrong ground and for the wrong reasons.

———

As we talked about earlier, in addition to wanting to have peace and joy, we want love. Our challenge is that we have such a distorted view of what love is. We confuse people pleasing for love; we think, on the one hand, that if we can just make people happy with us, they will feel loved, and we'll feel loved in return. That's a disastrous road. Jesus taught we are to love others from a place of being loved. He said, "You shall love your neighbor as yourself" (Matthew 22:39). It's that loving ourselves so we can love others that can get us all twisted up. Sometimes what *we* call "loving ourselves" can be self-serving or selfish. Sometimes we forget that Jesus modeled how to love others when He sacrificed Himself for us. On the other hand, operating out of people pleasing, even when some of those actions can look "good," isn't actually love for us or the other person at all.

Look, I get that this can be complicated stuff. It's convoluted and murky sometimes, trying to sift out the good and the bad. That's why I'm so glad we are on this journey together, where we'll look at God's design for community and connection and where we'll unpack the major areas where people pleasing snares us. We'll work on clearing up what has kept us confused. Taking an honest look at what drives us helps expose those dark places where we've been trapped—shining a light on how people pleasing has affected us.

The apostle Paul reminded us in Ephesians 5:13–15, "When anything is exposed by the light, it becomes visible, for anything that becomes visible is light. Therefore it says, 'Awake, O sleeper, and arise from the dead, and Christ will shine on you.' Look carefully then how you walk, not as unwise but as wise."

With God's help, you and I can wise up to how we've been living and learn a better way forward. Ultimately, we can get free from the twisted motives of people pleasing. For now, we're making important first steps. Our honesty—yours and mine—about how we got here, why we've been living as people pleasers, all begins to shine a light, and that light leads us to heal.

Let's Chat About It

You've spent this chapter thinking through a lot of questions, so I won't ask more here. What I would love for you to do is spend some time in the next day or two going back over your answers. Feel free to add more as things come to mind. This assessment doesn't have to be a one-and-done experience. As you think of how people pleasing has affected your life, you'll likely be reminded of different situations and experiences.

> Good and upright is the LORD;
> therefore he instructs sinners in the way.
> He leads the humble in what is right,
> and teaches the humble his way.
> All the paths of the LORD are steadfast love and
> faithfulness,
> for those who keep his covenant and his
> testimonies.
>
> PSALM 25:8–10

Chapter 3

WE NEED EACH OTHER BY BEAUTIFUL DESIGN

INTROVERT. EXTROVERT. SOMEWHERE IN BETWEEN. YOU and I, we've got different things about our personalities that make us unique. We might have different things that make us tick, different styles of music we prefer, different seasons of the year we like. You might be a night owl, while I'm more of an early bird. The things that make you laugh or cry could be different from the things that get to me.

But right in the middle of those things that make us unique is something all of us have: we're all drawn to other people.

Why is this? After all, it's people who can hurt us the most. It's people who are messy and inconvenient. It's people who break our hearts. It's people who start wars. It's people who often reject us and bring so much pain into our lives.

And yet we are still driven to be part of a community. We want to belong. As we talked about earlier, we want love, joy, and peace, and having other people in our lives is an important part of those drives. With all the risk that can be a part of human interaction, why are we still so drawn to others?

It's how we were created. It goes to the very core of how we were designed. Human connection goes beyond the desire to attend an occasional dinner party. It's a reflection of who God is. And because He created us in His image, it's our heartbeat too.

———

Here's something you don't want to sleep on. Should you find yourself in the southern Midwest, say, anywhere from south Kansas to western Missouri to Arkansas to Oklahoma to northern Texas, you're going to want to listen up: stop at a Braum's. Just trust me.

You'll have the best luck finding a location in Oklahoma because Oklahoma and Braum's go together like chocolate and shake, but we were fortunate enough to have one in the town where I grew up in northwest Arkansas. Braum's has burgers and fries and, yes, even a few grocery staples, but what they're really known for are their ice creams, shakes, and malts.

It's a whole thing.

The other place in our small town that was a big deal to me was Taco Bell. Because . . . Taco Bell.

But here's the thing: When I was growing up, we rarely ate out. The household budget was tiny, and the bills that come with raising a supersize family are huge, no matter how frugal you are. To get to go to one of these places was extra special. Getting to eat at Taco Bell was a rare delicacy and one that I never took for granted.

If you're wondering what else there is to do in northwest Arkansas other than hit up Braum's or Taco Bell, I have the answer for you, and it's actually amazing.

Broomball.

Don't knock it until you've tried it. Once a week or so, several of my siblings and I would head down to the local ice rink and battle it out with a bunch of other broomball warriors. Broomball is a lot like hockey, except without the skates, puck, helmets, pads, hockey sticks, or fistfights (at least usually, on the fistfights thing). Which pretty much sounds nothing like hockey, but it really is. You play in your tennis shoes on the ice and use a broomball stick to smack the ball into your team's net.

There were so many people who played broomball in my hometown. When we'd show up, we'd see tons of high schoolers and college-age kids and other homeschooled families. I'd hit the ice in my sneakers and my long skirt and would glide onto the frozen battlefield, finding that part of myself that was fearless and competitive.

I loved screaming around the ice as fast as my tennis shoes could slide, my muscles delighting at the burn, my brain searching for the next hole in the defense so I could slide and scurry toward the goal. It felt great to be out and to be moving.

And . . . it felt weird and awkward.

Everyone was perfectly nice. In addition to a lot of college kids, homeschooled families joined in each week. But they weren't homeschooled families like we were. The girls weren't out there trying to hit their stride while constricted in a long skirt. The families weren't showing up in a supersize bus like we were. They weren't sheltered with the intensity that we were. They all seemed, well, normal, while we seemed anything but.

After the weekly broomball matches, we'd leave the Jones Center, where the ice hockey rink was, and we'd gather at Braum's or Taco Bell to chat and laugh. A lot of the other families would also have dinner or snacks there. But our family's budget was really tight, which meant that, for my siblings and me, we could go to socialize but not for ice cream or tacos. Honestly, I was fine with it; I was happy to be out of the house and doing something athletic, decadent fast food or not.

This one night, the whole group went to Taco Bell after the game. Everyone was joking and talking. We were invited to sit at the table with a family with a few kids. The kids were in late high school and early college, and the dad liked playing broomball in our matches. They were so nice to us, so kind, asking us about ourselves, laughing and chatting.

And then came that awkward moment.

The parents got up to order food for their family, asking us if we wanted anything. Of course, we declined; we didn't have any money to spend, and we could eat dinner later at home. Sure, it made it a little weird for everyone, sitting with people who were eating their meals. It made me feel like we stood out even more . . . and we already stood out a lot, with the way we dressed and so many siblings in tow. Moments like this always made me remember just how many ways I didn't belong.

The mom and dad went to the counter and put in their order, then came back to the table, where they picked up the conversation. I took a deep breath, glad that the whole situation with the food ordering and us not getting anything was over.

After a few minutes, a server showed up at the table with several bags. And in those bags were Cinnamon Twists, a churro-type pastry. They smelled of butter, cinnamon, and warm sugar, and the perfume from those bags made my stomach swivel with a bolt of craving. I leaned back from the table a bit, not wanting that delicious scent to trigger my stomach to growl.

The mom and dad took the bags and started passing them around. "Here you go," they told me, handing me a bag.

I couldn't believe it.

They were sharing their Cinnamon Twists. With me. With us. With a tableful of sweaty kids in odd clothes, with nothing to offer. *I can't believe how nice they are*, I thought in wonder. *Why would they do this for us?* It made a huge impression on me, that people would want to befriend me and do kind things for me, even though I felt so uncouth and out of the loop, like I hadn't worked hard enough to gain their acceptance and friendship.

But what they were extending to me was a little snapshot of what makes human community so special, so transformational, when it's healthy and when it serves others. I think part of why this memory had such an impression on me is that it stands out as an experience of the simplest and best moments of how we should be toward each other—nothing to gain, no one to impress, just a need met and a kindness given. Their kindness was a small thing with a big message: we need each other by beautiful design.

Never underestimate the perspective-bending power of sharing your Cinnamon Twists.

———

Have you heard of super-agers? These are people who live into their eighties and nineties and beyond with vitality and spark. Their memories and cognitive skills remain sharp, far better than many of their same-age colleagues. Researchers and physicians have been looking at these people, trying to understand what makes them stay so vibrant in the face of aging. And guess what they've figured out? Yep. Super-agers are super social.[1] It's one of the top things researchers find when they look at the similarities of super-agers. Not their daily diets. Not their histories. Not their finances or medical care or vitamin regimen. It's their connection to other people. They remain very engaged in their communities. They have people over. They have deep conversations. They care for people, and people care for them. And somehow, all the way to the cellular level, it makes a difference in not only how long they live but *how* they live.[2]

Why would we see evidence of this, cell deep?

It all goes back to the beginning of the Bible, where we learn about God creating us.

In the very first book of the Bible, in the first few chapters of Genesis, we learn about how God created humans. He considers us the crowning achievement of all His incredible creation, the one creation that was made in His image (1:27).

After the creation of the universe and the stars and the sun and the planets and all the creatures and plants, God created Adam, formed him from the dust of the ground. God had created the perfect place for Adam to live. He gave him the perfect job, which was to name all the animals and to manage all that God had created on the earth. He gave him the perfect organic grocery store in the form of a perfect garden, with all kinds of fresh fruits and vegetables always available. There was the perfect irrigation system, with a beautiful river flowing through the garden of Eden. In everything that Adam could need, God had it covered.

Except for one thing.

"Then the LORD God said, 'It is not good that the man should be alone; I will make him a helper fit for him'" (Genesis 2:18).

God saw that Adam needed companionship, that while there were all these good things readily available, supplying whatever Adam could need, there was not another person for Adam to do life with. So God put Adam into a deep sleep, took one of his ribs, and created a woman, Eve, for him (vv. 21–22).

Why would God do that?

Because God created Adam in His image. And God exists in community. The Father, the Son, and the Holy Spirit are the three members of the Trinity. Which means that God has, for all eternity, existed in relationship! And the relationship in the Godhead between the Father, Son, and Spirit is one of unity and love. It's a spectacular, cosmic, mysterious snapshot of a Being who exists in perfect relationship. So, when God made Adam in His image, of course He made Adam for relationship just like his Creator.

God, in the earliest days of our story with Him, created us for community. He doesn't stop creating until that person-to-person experience exists.

———

It's said that when you're learning a second language, some of the hardest things to learn are the sayings and humor used by that culture; you can know that you're becoming truly fluent in a different language when you start to get the jokes and the metaphors. Well, I have an additional theory about being fluent in a language, and that's knowing the movies and music that create a lot of the cultural references in that language.

This, given my extremely sheltered background, means there are times in a group of people when I feel like I'm not even speaking the same language. I saw very few movies and listened to very little music other than hymns and classical compositions when I was a kid. So there are times when I'm chatting and laughing with a group when someone brings up a line from a movie or busts out with a lyric from a popular song, and I'm left there thinking, *Huh?* It's always a weird moment for me, feeling like I'm the only one who doesn't get it.

So you can imagine that when I'd hear Jeremy on occasion holler, "Willlllssssssoooooonnnn!" I needed some context.

Here's the upside of being so behind in my cinematic and Top 40 pop hits education: there are so many great movies out there that I'm now getting to experience. Oscar winners, comedies, epic fantasies—they're all new and thrilling for me. Jeremy is often my tour guide, bringing me up to speed on all kinds of awesome stories and introducing me to music that I'm hearing for the first time.

If you dip back into the year 2000, you'll find a masterpiece in the movie vault starring Tom Hanks. In the movie *Cast Away*, he plays Chuck Noland, a business executive who lives by his packed calendar and intense ambitions. Things go awry when, on a business trip, his plane crashes over the ocean. After crawling into a life raft in the midst of the horrific storm that took the plane down, Chuck washes ashore on an island somewhere in the Pacific, the only survivor of the accident.

The movie follows Chuck as he deals with his first days of trying to survive, thinking rescue is imminent. It then shows Chuck as the realization sets in that he is all alone and that the rescue he's so desperately hoped for isn't coming. He becomes depressed. He considers taking his own life. He is in deep despair.

And that's when he meets Wilson.

Okay, *meets* is a little strong. A volleyball from the wreckage washes up on the beach of Chuck's deserted island. One day, Chuck badly cuts his hand while trying to start a fire, and, in his anger, he starts throwing things, including the volleyball. The bloody handprint his hand leaves on the volleyball looks something like a face with a shock of hair, and in his loneliness, Chuck adopts the volleyball as a friend. He names him Wilson in honor of the volleyball manufacturer brand.

Wilson is Chuck's closest friend and confidante for the next several years. Wilson's arrival is a significant turning point in Chuck's experience. Wilson becomes critical to his survival. Sure, you could reduce the storyline down to saying it's about a guy and his volleyball, but I'm telling you, it's a story that will destroy your mascara and leave you in puddles of an ugly cry. It's such an incredible example of the bone-deep need we have as humans for companionship and the lengths we will go to to create those relationships, even when all we have available is a volleyball. It shows that we can have the basic sustenance we need to support our physical lives, like food and water and shelter, but that we can't live, truly live, without others in our lives.

The list of ways we're wired for human connection goes on and on. People who aren't connected to others have higher rates of depression and cardiovascular disease. They grapple with anxiety and are at greater risk for strokes.[3] When we have healthy relationships with others, we feel like we belong. We get bursts of happy brain chemicals when we help other people, share our resources, give hugs. To be human is to seek out other humans, to break bread and share life and shoulder each other's burdens.

Needing other people is normal. It's baked into who we are. And God is the Baker.

Sadly, this perfect community that began in the garden of Eden would not stay so perfect. Soon, the relational bliss Adam and Eve enjoyed was shattered as sin entered the picture. When Adam and Eve defied God and ate the fruit He had told them not to eat, immediately relational tension was introduced. They once walked with God, enjoying His presence with no reason to be ashamed. But now? They hid from Him (Genesis 3:8). A relationship that had been one of pure delight and joy was now filled with shame. Even the relationship between Adam and Eve broke down, as they blamed each other (v. 12). The result of their sin was anger, brokenness, and division.

We were made for community. The God of community created us in His image to delight in and enjoy Him and one another. But sin corrupts. It corrupted the relationship of our first parents, and it continues to corrupt ours today. Not only is our relationship with God, our Creator, broken because of sin, but our relationships with other people are broken. If we are going to have any hope of repairing and returning to a place of thriving relationships, we need to make things right with our Creator.

———

"Hey, can I talk to you?" he casually asked.

"Sure," Jeremy responded to him. Stepping aside to find a quiet place out of the hustle and bustle of a crowded room, Jeremy asked, "What's up?"

The guy, who was an acquaintance and who Jeremy would see around from time to time, got right to the point. And it wasn't what Jeremy was expecting.

"You know, I've noticed how you look at me when I see you, like you're bothered by me and look down on me."

Jeremy was completely taken aback. Aside from knowing his name, Jeremy didn't know anything about this guy. When Jeremy would see him, he'd greet him kindly and usually share some small talk. But this felt completely out of the blue.

Not sure what to say, Jeremy shared with him that he hadn't felt that way toward him and certainly was not trying to communicate that in how he did or didn't look at him. Jeremy walked away from that conversation baffled, sharing with me later how he was trying to process how on earth that guy came to the conclusions he did.

For this guy, what he imagined coming from Jeremy was judgment and arrogance. He felt diminished and anxious. He clearly had put a lot of thought and energy and hurt feelings into what he believed Jeremy thought of him. But for Jeremy? Whenever he'd see that guy around, he hadn't thought any of those things!

I tell you the story of this encounter because I can so relate to the guy who approached Jeremy. While I haven't had the courage to initiate that kind of conversation, I've certainly built all kinds of narratives in my head about how I think other people perceive me and what they think of me. I did it back in that little apartment in Laredo, visualizing all kinds of imagined responses from our upcoming guests. I did it when I was a kid, worried about what people would think who saw my siblings and me out in public after our television show started. I'm certainly no mind reader, but boy have I thought myself one when it comes to my worries about what other people might be thinking about me.

That's the side of the blade of being made for human connection. I can get so spooled up about trying to manage imaginary conversations in my head that it can keep me from actually being present with people. I'm projecting myself out into the future, speculating what their dialogue with their spouse will be after our dinner party or small group or double date.

When you're a people pleaser, you're more likely than not writing scripts for other people in your head. *All. The. Time.*

There's a quote I love that speaks to this: "You probably wouldn't worry about what people think of you if you could know how seldom they do."[4]

Now, you and I both know that a lot of the time, we likely call it wrong. Just like the guy who confronted Jeremy, we might think people think about us a lot more than they actually do. But let's face it: there are certain groups of people who *are* talking about you or judging you. It's a unique kind of hurt when you find out that you have been the topic of judgy conversation among your friends. Or maybe they're even saying it straight to your face, piling on their opinions on how you're spending your time, what you're wearing, or how they're unhappy with you.

When you're a people pleaser like me, what's your response to finding out that someone has been talking behind your back? For a person who's breaking free of people pleasing, it probably looks like recognizing that person may be untrustworthy and unkind. But when I'm sliding back into my people-pleasing tendencies, I might find myself spinning like an electric meter on a hot summer day, trying to figure out how, *how*, to get back on the right side of these people's opinions. The same goes for someone who unfairly critiques me to my face. When I'm operating from a people-pleasing base, gaining back the approval of naysayers becomes a dominating goal in my life. I might work harder, smile bigger, adjust all kinds of things I'm doing and saying, just to get back on their good side.

But that isn't the only response I've had. Yes, sometimes it's been to scramble even harder to fix things, but sometimes it's been to shut myself off from people completely. Honestly, there are always

When you're a people pleaser, you're more likely than not writing scripts for other people in your head. All. The. Time.

going to be risks involved in any kind of human interaction, and we can find ourselves flipping over that double-edged sword, back and forth, trying to use the blade of avoidance to cut through the noise in our hearts. I've gone to that extreme as well.

In my own quest to break free from my toxic people-pleasing tendencies, this is an area where I've severely overcorrected at times. *I can't handle trying to keep everyone happy anymore*, I'd think. *I'll just avoid people altogether. That'll fix it. Then I won't have to deal with it.*

But guess what? Avoiding people or emotionally cutting yourself off from community as a way to cure your people pleasing is a temporary Band-Aid at best. What lies beneath is a splinter of fear that's going to continue to infect your heart. Patch it up any way you want, but there comes a day when that splinter begins to inflame and infect all kinds of relationships, just like it did for me when I moved to Laredo.

Overcompensating isn't the answer. And neither is isolating yourself. You were made for people, and people were made for you. To accept anything less is to cut yourself off from one of God's great blessings.

Let's Chat About It

Community is a big word in our culture today, and while the term may have become familiar, I don't think that we've really landed on exactly what we're talking about when we use the word. It seems like we all bring different expectations and hoped-for outcomes to experiences of community. Sometimes we find what we think we're looking for, and sometimes we don't.

1. What is a community experience that turned out differently than you thought it would?
2. Have you ever considered that you were made by God to enjoy relationship with Him *and* other people?
3. How do you think we can be restored to a right relationship with God?
4. Have you ever considered that you were created for community? Do you find that easy to believe or not? Why?
5. Who is someone in your life who seems to have the healthy kind of connection and community God created us for?
6. What are some expectations you've had for relationships and community that you're now thinking might not be the healthiest?
7. With God knowing that sin so often makes community difficult, why do you think He still intends us to be connected? Why do you think He created us to need each other?

Chapter 4

DESPERATE IS NOT
A GOOD LOOK

ZAP!!!

One minute Joe was hanging out with his friend, and the next, he was in crazy pain. He'd touched an electric wire fence and got jolted into next week.

But this was no accident.

At the edge of our property, there lived a boy who was the same age as my little brother Joe, no more than six or seven years old. Joe immediately wanted this kid to like him. He watched everything he did and tried to copy his swagger. This kid would clear his throat and spit, and the next thing you knew, Joe was doing it just like him. (You should have seen my mom's face the first time he did it, when, out of nowhere, Joe spat on the ground in front of her.

"What in the world are you doing, son?" she asked him, eyes wide. "Spittin'," he answered. Spittin' in this phase of Joe's life equaled the very definition of cool.)

From the way he walked to the way he talked, the way this neighbor boy showed up in the world became the template Joe was always trying to copy.

And this boy was big energy, rambunctious, and always, always daring Joe to do crazier and crazier things. For a while, they went through a phase where this kid would say, "Okay, Joe, I'm going to think up a trick or a dare I want you to do, and if you don't do it, you have to pay me money." Joe, because he was desperate to have this kid think that he was cool, would agree to this questionable investment strategy. And, you guessed it, this kid would come up with something so outlandish or dangerous or dumb or all three that Joe couldn't or wouldn't do it, which, somehow, some way, meant that Joe owed this kid part of his hard-earned money.

Joe was *so* desperate to be this kid's friend.

Which brings us to the day that Joe got zapped by the electric fence. The neighbor kid dared Joe to touch the fence. Joe was already down some serious dollars from not being able to complete a previous set of dares, and he wasn't about to lose anymore. So touch the fence he did. And when Joe did, and he got zapped, the kid laughed and said, "Ha! Got you!" Joe was wailing in pain, tears in his eyes, humiliated in front of this kid he so badly wanted to befriend.

Did Joe know the fence was electric? Yep. That fence was on our property to keep the cows on their side of the line. Had we been warned what would happen if any of us touched an electric fence? Also yes.

Did the desperation to have the approval of the cool kid across the property line trump all that Joe knew about the electric fence and the consequences of said fence?

Yep.

That's how the desperation of people pleasing works. Even when you know you're going to get zapped, you'll do something anyway, all in a reckless bid to maybe, just maybe, get someone to think you're worth knowing.

———

When I was thinking about the title for this chapter, I kept coming back to the word *desperate*. That's because the word *desperate* just hits right in the bullseye for me when it comes to describing how I've often felt in all my efforts and attempts to keep everyone happy in my life. I've been desperate for friends, desperate for approval, desperate to avoid conflict, desperate for peace, desperate for rest.

But then I had to ask myself: What does the word *desperate* mean? And where did the word come from?

A little internet search gave me some answers. As it turns out, the word *desperate* comes from the Latin root word for being in despair, for being *hopeless*.[1] I hadn't thought about desperation before in that way, but boy, did it connect. At the height of my people pleasing, I was battling the sense of being hopeless that people could like me for just being me. I was in despair that I wasn't enough for Jeremy, for my community, and even for God. And when you feel like hope is fleeting, you'll do all kinds of desperate things to try to hang on to the line that keeps you from going entirely over the edge.

Then there was the next part of the definition: "without care for safety, extremely rash, driven to recklessness by despair." Of course, visions of Joe touching that electric fence popped into my head. That was certainly an act that didn't factor in any kind of safety standard. But it also got me thinking about the times when my own desperation pushed me beyond reasonable limits. Or the times I didn't get the sleep I needed, either worrying about what everyone might think or reorganizing a cabinet just in case the friend coming over for coffee the next day might just maybe, perhaps, open that cabinet and be horrified by the jumbled shelves. I've been so desperate for the positive opinions of others that I've responded by going to the opposite extreme, all the way over to isolating myself. And when I go to isolation, I stop serving as Christ would have me serve. My primary focus becomes self-preservation and selfishness, a core of self-serving caution.

When I interact with community from a position of desperation, what should be a beautiful, mutually beneficial, other-oriented space becomes an on-demand grab for what I can get from you, how I need you to make me feel, and what I'll do to try to get that from you.

In thinking about what *desperate* means and where it came from, it makes me consider the meaning behind my own desperate measures to please. On the one hand, I really do like serving people, helping others, making people feel comfortable. Obviously, those things aren't wrong; in fact, they're good. It's like that electric fence. It was a good thing for keeping the cows safe on the property. But on the other hand, just like how taking a dare about an electric fence can be a bad thing, it's not lost on me that I far too often have either pulled back from being with others or tried to control their perception of me, and all of that has zapped me of peace.

———

Mary and Martha and their brother Lazarus lived in a little town just south of Jerusalem called Bethany. From what we can tell from Scripture when these siblings are mentioned, Jesus had a friendship with them, the kind of friendship that was close enough that Jesus was comfortable dropping by their house one evening for dinner with all His disciple buddies in tow.

Now, the way I've always heard it told, Martha was spinning around trying to get everything ready for her guests while her sister Mary was hanging out in the living room, listening to Jesus talk. Martha finally had enough of this situation, being the one who was getting all the things ready for all the people, and she finally lost her cool, demanding that Jesus make Mary help her: "Martha was distracted with much serving. She came to him and asked, 'Lord, do you not care that my sister has left me to serve alone? Tell her then to help me'" (Luke 10:40).

Jesus reminded Martha that she was all wound up about all kinds of things but that, really, at the end of the day, there are only a few things in life that are that important. He said, "Mary has chosen the good portion, which will not be taken away from her" (v. 42). Mary chose to spend time listening to Jesus, to spend time with Him, instead of getting frenzied over details.

When I heard this story when I was younger, I always focused on the worker-bee mentality of Martha and the chill attitude of Mary and how Jesus responded to those things. The takeaway for me was that it was better to calm down and hang out than to get panicked about the house and the food and the party favors and if the guest bathroom had enough toilet paper. But I'll be the first to admit, as much as I wanted to see things Mary's way, to take a beat and a pause and simply rest at the feet of Jesus, Martha's situation seemed far more familiar to me. Panicked about house and food and toilet paper supplies is my natural state. Trying to make everything perfect.

In many ways, I homed in on the part of the story where it almost sounds like Martha got scolded for trying to be a good hostess. So, me being me, I set myself up for a cycle of failure, scolding myself for even trying to be a good hostess (or student or friend or for being conscientious in general) while also scolding myself for *failing* to be a good hostess (or whatever other role I was trying to fill).

Now, I get that when you go looking for connections, you'll

often find them, and given that I'm pretty deep into the unpacking of this whole issue of people pleasing, I'm more likely than not to find shades of people pleasing all around me. But I seem to kick off at this whole idea of having people over; you can imagine that Martha's story carries a different weight for me now.

When I go back into the verses, I'm struck by this detail at the beginning of this passage: It's Martha who initially invited Jesus and the disciples to come over. It's Martha who took the initiative to create this cozy community space where people could hear Jesus teach and hang out and relax.

And then, it's Martha who got angry when people did exactly that, especially her sister.

I've been that girl. My particular blend of it is a heavy focus on perfectionism. I've tried to do everything with a self-imposed standard of perfection, so that no one could judge me, then resented what it's cost me in time and energy. I've worn myself out chasing others' opinions, desperate for their love and attention that I'm trying to buy with all my good deeds and sacrifice. I *recognize* Martha. I can see a scenario where Martha desperately wanted to be on everyone's good side by hosting the Jesus dinner party. She wanted her house to look great because she didn't want anyone to think she was a hot mess. She wanted the food to be perfect, the ambience to be just right, because, if it wasn't, what would the Bethany neighbors think? What might the disciples have said afterward if she burned the bread and didn't use her best fabric napkins?

For Martha, it's possible that the stakes seemed so high, that the need to please these people who were important to her meant so much, that she lost the thread.

And came unraveled.

Then there's Jesus' reaction. I always assumed that people were ready to tsk-tsk-tsk me if I couldn't make everything perfect, because I thought that everyone was at the ready to show me all the places I'd missed a spot. So I unintentionally put that tone on how Jesus talked to Martha. But when I look deeper, I see something far better, far kinder, than my original filter would allow. Jesus wasn't saying that all Martha's work and worry wasn't valuable. No, He said that it was *needed*. But He gave Martha a scale to measure her distractions by.

That's the beautiful, balanced perspective that Jesus brings to our lives. He reassured Martha that she mattered, that what mattered to her mattered. She wasn't wrong for wanting to do things well, for wanting to serve others well. What Jesus asked her to evaluate was the *why* behind what she was doing, and the scale of the thing.

Here's what strikes me: I think Martha was so busy trying to buy friendship that she was missing the friendship and community literally hanging out in her living room. (Here I am again, having to raise my hand.) She made the weight of all her tasks so heavy that she was crushed under the resulting anxiety. (And my hand goes up again.) All that made her attitude one of desperate frustration. Interrupting Jesus mid-conversation, griping that the people *she* invited to her house had required all kinds of chores on her part. Desperate activity. Desperate blaming.

And let's face it; desperate is not a good look.

———

I've seen it play out many times before. You probably have too. You're part of a church or volunteer group or your kids' school parent group. And there's that one person or that couple who are super involved. They're at every event. They open their home multiple nights a week so the youth group kids can hang out. They spend weeks and weeks building sets for the school fall festival. Whatever the need is, they're there, out-serving, out-volunteering, out-working everyone else.

All that serving seems amazing and noble and all the things, but usually, you don't have to scratch too far beneath the surface to find that there are leaks and mold. There's that couple always serving the youth and young adults at church, but then you find out their own family life with their own kids is falling apart. There's that mom spending all her time with the school-parent organization while her child is deeply struggling with a learning challenge and badly needs his mom's focus and help. There's the colleague who takes on organizing the spring fun run, but she hasn't slept in months and is just a few weeks away from a health crisis.

A friend of mine recently called these kinds of people *serial servers*. I like that.

Like I said, I typically go to isolating myself when it comes to my own people-pleasing methods, but I've also served from the wrong heart, the wrong motive, at times.

Serial serving can be hard to identify because, from the outside, it looks so good! You get all kinds of accolades and praise. But on the inside, some of the most important responsibilities you have get dropped in the pursuit of all that altruism. You see it in the stories of pastors' kids. You see it in the saying, "The cobbler's children have no shoes." That's not to say that everyone who volunteers and works at a varsity level is going to have a cautionary tale on the home front, with their marriage or kids. Some people do seem to have a supernatural ability to lead and serve and only sleep on occasion, and my hat is off to them. But for most of us, every single thing we say yes to means there's something we're saying no to. We don't like that math, so we ignore it, but the results still come for us anyway.

In no way do I judge people for the serial serving situations they get themselves into; I've gotten myself into plenty of jams like these. All these people are intending to do good. They want to make a difference. And, hey, as people trying to build good lives and help out our fellow human beings, aren't these activities what we should be focusing on?

But you have to ask: At what cost?

When we first moved to California, we lived in a beautiful house really close to the seminary campus where Jeremy was working on his masters in divinity and also on staff at the church. Convenient? Absolutely. But we also wanted to purchase our own home. So, when a friend contacted us about a home that had gone on the market and was a reasonable commute for Jeremy's schooling and work, we jumped on it. We were thrilled when we went to see the house and realized it was exactly what we'd been looking for.

But once again, I found myself packing up, leaving behind what had become familiar, and needing to create new routines and rhythms and community.

Do you sense a theme here? It's almost like God's been trying to teach me something.

Add into that mix having a toddler and a baby, and you get a pretty good picture of what tired—that deep-in-your-bones kind of tired—looks like. But I wanted to make friends in my new town. I wanted to have other moms and kids in my life.

So when I found out that my friend Erin and her little baby lived near our new neighborhood, I immediately invited her over. She showed up at the time we'd agreed. Yes, I'd tried to clear the sink of dishes, and I'd fluffed and chopped a couple of pillows on the couch. The house wasn't *quite* up to my usual standards, but I was out of energy and time when the doorbell rang.

Erin came in with her darling baby on her hip. As my kids started running up the stairs and pulling out toys, Erin and I stood in the kitchen, chatting. As we chatted, Erin's baby, Eden, started to get restless, so Erin put her on the floor to play. Eden started crawling around, her chubby knees churning across the floor to explore all the things.

That's when it happened. I turned around for a moment to grab a cup of water, and Erin was in the middle of telling me a story. I turned back around, looked down . . . and saw baby Eden under the kitchen table, shoving Cheerios that she'd found under my daughters' chairs in her mouth at lightning speed.

And believe me, that baby was faassssssstttt. Floor Cheerios. So. Gross.

It felt like the clock stopped for a few seconds until my panic mode clicked. *Oh no!* I was internally freaking out. I couldn't believe I'd forgotten to sweep the floor one more time before Erin arrived. *I'm such a terrible housekeeper,* my inner dialogue raged. *Why would anyone want to come over to my house if they can't even put their baby down to crawl?* These were all the thoughts racing through my head in a split second, even as I was trying to form words to say out loud to warn Erin about her dusty Cheerio-eating under-the-table baby. *That's it. Friendship over before it starts.*

But before I could even say anything, Erin looked down, saw what her baby was up to, and started laughing. "Found you a snack, huh?" she grinned. Baby Eden smiled up at her and grabbed another piece of cereal off the floor. Erin casually bent down and picked her up, all the while continuing the story she'd been telling me.

Wait, what?

What had just happened?

"I'm so sorry about that!" I stammered. "I can't believe I didn't get those swept up! Is the baby okay—are you okay?"

I was waiting for the disapproving look or the run to the kitchen sink to scrub down the baby, or the screaming wrestling match of trying to dig Cheerios out of the baby's mouth. Instead, what I found was . . . friendship. And grace. And perspective.

She gave me a gentle smile. "Of course! That's how it is at my house too. We've got little kids, babies. You're not true friends until your kids eat each other's leftover cereal off the floor, am I right?" And then she jumped back into the rest of the story she'd been telling me.

Talk about a gift.

She wasn't mad. She wasn't shocked. She wasn't judging me. She wasn't bolting from the house, slathering her baby in hand sanitizer, threatening never to return. Nope. She was there, in my less-than-perfect house, in my Cheerio-confetti kitchen, to be my friend. Not my judge, not my critic, not my correction squad. She wasn't daring me to touch the electric fence of perfection in order to become her friend. As a matter of fact, she saw this moment of mom-reality as the bonding agent for friendship.

That's when I realized that there was something I wanted even more than a polished reputation.

I want *real*. Real relationships. Real freedom. Real conversations and real connection.

I realize that you might not have as many mind-spiraling internal freak-out issues with floor Cheerios as I do. But what I've learned among my fellow people pleasers is that we've all got *something*. Maybe yours is feeling like you have to be perfectly put together before you walk out the door, just in case you run into people you know. Maybe yours is how you present yourself on social media. Perhaps it has to do with showing up for your kid's soccer match with all the mom swag and the perfect organic, nutritious snacks. We've all got some forward-facing thing that breaks us out in a cold sweat when we don't feel like we've kept up the facade as well as we intended.

I get that you're desperate to be accepted, to show up well, desperate to simply not embarrass yourself. But I'm here to tell you that deep down, like me, just on the other side of all that desperate, there's what you really want—something that means much more.

I want people in my life who really know me, who truly love me. I want that for you too. Even though in the past I've been willing to touch a proverbial electric fence to try to make someone like me, now what I want far more is people in my life who remind me that my value is not in taking every dare or demand—that they love me regardless. That my worth isn't in how clean my house is, how put together I look, or if my kids are perfectly behaved or having a raging case of toddler tantrums. I've spent far too long trying to cement friendships together with the flaky, crumbly mortar of smooth flawlessness. But it's the grit in life that creates the friction for things to stick. Yes, even grit like floor Cheerios.

Hear me out: What if, instead of trying to do all the things to make you the cool girl, the cool wife, the cool mom, poreless and Teflon, you went for a little bit of texture?

What if you and I stopped *pretending*?

That's the part about people pleasing that's taken me a long time to see. All that effort? So much of it was pretending. Pretending to be enthusiastic about signing up for one more thing, even though inside I was exhausted. Pretending to not have an opinion so I wouldn't rock the boat. Pretending to be the easygoing one instead of having some legit preferences. All that pretending is the batter of burnout. Yes, you can get burned-out from the tasks you take on in your efforts to manage others' opinions of you, but at the base of it, every time, is pretending to be someone you're not.

It reminds me of Proverbs 13:7, which says, "One pretends to be rich, yet has nothing."

It seems to me there are two speeds when it comes to the pretending part of people pleasing. In my case, I got so worn down that I just stopped. I stopped trying to make friends; I stopped risking not being able to control the outcomes. The other side of it is having to escalate the level of pretend to try and maintain the results you think you're getting. Full stop and avoid or full steam ahead: those seem to be the only two settings in the people-pleasing pretend game.

Okay, I get it. Maybe it feels a little strong, that word *pretend*. I confess, if someone had lovingly confronted me with that word a few years ago, I would have pushed back. Probably not out loud. After all, I had an image to uphold. But inside, I would have thought,

What if you and I
stopped pretending?

Hey! That's not fair! I'm out here trying to do all the things, and you're over there, lounging around, acting like it's my problem!

All that pretending is part of the sin nature of people pleasing. I know, I know, it's on trend to avoid using words like *sin* these days. We don't want to shame anyone. We want to be known for our love and mercy and grace. But consider this: calling out sin can be an act of love and mercy and grace. Jesus does it all the time in Scripture. He does it because He knows that we can't have freedom if we can't see what binds us.

Pretending in the way I'm talking about is sin because it's not honest; it's a lie. It's a lie that we use to influence and control the reactions, responses, and feelings of others. Yes, we're helping at our kids' school because being engaged with our kids' educational community is a good thing, is a neighborly thing. But when you and I do it so people will think we're good moms or so maybe our kids will get invited to the right birthday parties, we're deep into pretending territory. People-pleasing pretending has this weird economy to it; we give out all kinds of parts of ourselves in a pay-to-play, give-to-get scheme, expecting to get people's love and respect and approval as part of the effort.

And when we don't get it, and we have that burned-out, complaining, weepy experience? That is when the sin of all that pretending shows up in Technicolor.

I've identified another place of wrongdoing in my people pleasing. I began to realize it when I paid attention to what I said to myself about how it felt to be out-serving, overscheduling, and under-resting. It showed up in that inner talk with phrases like:

After all I've done for them . . .

I can't believe they didn't seem all that appreciative . . .

Why am I the only one who is back here in the fellowship hall washing all the dishes and keeping the food hot?

As hard as it can be to admit this, I was being pretty transactional. I was giving to get. Ugh. That's hard to confess, but I can't deny it when I look at my inner dialogue. I was trying to buy friendship with my good deeds. I was trying to get a certain response out of people by all my do-gooding, whether that be the perception I wanted them to have of me, or their willingness to help me in some way, or any other type of acknowledgment I wanted from them.

There's a word for it, and boy, do I not like it. But here it is: *manipulation*. When we do something with an expectation that it will drive someone's behavior or emotion the way we want it to, when we do something with a high calculation that it will get us what we want, that's manipulation. I think that's where all the burnout and resentment and frustration started to really build up in me because I was doing all this stuff, thinking there would be a return.

Is it wrong to hope that the efforts you're putting into something will make someone feel special or valued or appreciated? Of course not. But when there's a tail on that hope, that not only will they feel special or valued or appreciated, but they'll also think you're the best and the kindest and the most perfect, well, then, Houston, we have a problem.

Which takes us right back to that story about Mary and Martha. Scripture doesn't say exactly what Martha hoped to get out of her hostess-with-the-mostest efforts when she had Jesus and the boys over for dinner. But because of my own journey, I can now spot her clear signs of overwhelm and frustration in the biblical account when she complained to Jesus. Whatever she was hoping to get out of the pretend, pay-to-play game, she wasn't getting it, and that led to an epic tattletale situation on her sister and some needed words from Jesus to get her back on track: "Martha, Martha, you are anxious and troubled about many things, but one thing is necessary" (Luke 10:41–42).

What *is* necessary? It's listening to Jesus. It's learning of His love, His wisdom, His compassion and mercy. It's finding forgiveness and fulfillment in His grace. When that truth is embraced first, it makes all the other stuff begin to fall into the right places.

———

Parenting, marriage, community—it all puts you and me in a position to work, work, work, clean, clean, clean, to do everything so we can be seen as valuable, as wanted. But over time, because we do all these because of what we need to get out of them, we can grow feelings of resentment and bitterness. *No one appreciates me. No one cares about all the work I'm putting in. No one approves of what I'm doing. I'm not getting what I wanted out of this deal!*

Even though it looks like we're taking care of everybody else, it's still driven by a motive of self-gratification. It's not a picture of how we were designed to be. It is the way that we've been tricked by the Enemy to try to get our needs met. Should people give us approval and gratitude when we bless and serve and love them? Of course! But when the main reason we're doing those things is for what we can get, we're going to get shocked in the heart again and again.

As a mom, wife, friend, author, and media person with a busy schedule, I get run down. You do too. Sometimes you need to recognize you're being drained. We don't get extra bonus points for pushing our schedules and our responsibilities to the very limit. But often the issue with a sense of burnout is motivation. What's driving you, what's driving me, to drive so hard?

Approval seeking is a tough, unforgiving, and unfair taskmaster.

I keep a close eye on myself these days, when requests and obligations, events and opportunities begin darting across my email and calendar. If I forget the "necessary thing," asking God first for direction into how to spend my days, all the "many things" are quick to get me anxious and troubled. But when I start from a position of knowing that I'm not in a race to get God or anyone else to accept me, that because of Jesus God takes me just as I am, I can take on serving others from a place of genuine joy, not pretended pep wrapped in potential disappointment.

Ask yourself this in your own efforts:

Are you pretending to be excited or joyful about whatever task or project you're doing?

Are you pretending to be someone you're not?

Do you have an expectation of payback for how you're serving someone?

Do you find yourself feeling shortchanged if someone doesn't respond to you the way you hoped after you do something for them?

I want to challenge you to let go of the many things that make up your "desperate for something better."

What if you swap *desperate* for its opposite, *hopeful*?

Hopeful to make some new friends, with pure motives (and no electric fence dares).

Hopeful to have people in your life who value you for who you *are*, not just what you *do*.

Hopeful to love people well because you have also learned to love and appreciate yourself.

Hopeful to love people well without an agenda for building up your own self-esteem and self-worth.

If a friendship, relationship, or community makes you feel so desperate to be a part of it that you must perform and produce and perfect in order to be accepted, can I just tell you? Run. It's an electric fence not worth scaling. Any relationship that begins on that basis is likely to fail. At the very least, it will always make you feel small. You'll get zapped when you least expect it—and even when you do, I'm here to tell you that more than you want to be part of that sorority of the electric fence, you want to be known. To be loved. To be treasured. To be appreciated for just who you are. And when you let go of desperate, you'll find the freedom that's just on the other side of that fence.

Let's Chat About It

It's wild to think about the ways we try to win others' approval and friendship. While there are lots of great people in the world who would love to be in community with you, there are also those who, for whatever reason, will expect you to jump through all kinds of hoops . . . and you and I, as people pleasers, will often do it. That desperation for all the things our hearts are hungry for can get us into some wild situations.

1. What is something you've done for someone's approval or good opinion of you that left you feeling zapped?
2. What is it that you've been feeling desperate for? What are you longing for that doesn't feel fulfilled?
3. What do you feel like you've been pretending at?

Let's finish out this chapter together with this verse from Proverbs. There are healthy ways for us to find soul contentment, and then there are ways that are self-serving and selfish. We're going to continue to look at the difference, but know for now that God longs for you to feel whole.

> *Hope deferred makes the heart sick, but*
> *a desire fulfilled is a tree of life.*
> PROVERBS 13:12

Chapter 5

TRADING DOWN

THE PHONE RANG ON A RANDOM TUESDAY, AND I picked up to find another new friend on the line. We had gotten to know each other at church. She'd share a little bit of her story with me when we would see each other at church services and events. Her life experience was a tough and heartbreaking one, and I knew that she was looking for help and insight. My heart really went out to her, but I felt a little pull to hold back a bit.

At the beginning of the call, we did the typical opening banter, *good good fine fine*. And then her voice dropped a little, became quieter and unsure.

"Hey, Jinger," she asked, "would you have some time for us to talk? I've got something going on that I could really use your thoughts on. I could run by your house. It's something really personal."

Her request hung in the air, caught somewhere between her courageous vulnerability and a swirl of thoughts in my head.

Here I was, someone trying to develop relationships with people in our church, my husband a pastor, and I have to tell you, I hesitated. And stalled. My mind immediately went to all the ways it was going to cost me if I said yes. I'd have to open my home, with the mess of family life scattered everywhere. I'd have to open my own heart. To help her, I'd have to be open about my own challenges and failures. And then what would she think of me?

The natural thing to do would be to invite her over. It was midday on a relatively open weekday. But why did I pause? Because of the toys on the floor in the living room. Because of my own uncertainty of how to help. Because of the potential of compromising my own sense of security if I didn't appear perfectly wise and put together. Because I was nervous. Because I didn't know if I would have the answers. Because of fear.

And there I stood, phone in hand, ready to trade down the possibility of investing in someone's life to protect my own sense of safety and control.

———

I'm not alone in my temptation to trade down. At times you've probably also risked missing out on doing the better thing, the right thing. One story in Scripture shows me that this tendency to trade down is something many of us fight.

He was the oldest in a set of fraternal twins. His name was Esau, and his twin's name was Jacob.

Sometimes twins are pretty similar in their personalities, whether they're fraternal or identical. I have two sets of twins among my siblings, both sets fraternal. Each set of twins does have a sweet bond and friendship. And while they don't have any kind of wild connection like reading each other's minds or anything like that, they have some things in common personality-wise that remind me of each of them.

But this guy and his twin? They were about as different as you can get. Esau loved all things outdoors and hunting and fishing. The younger twin, Jacob, preferred to hang out on the home front. Esau was more impulsive. Jacob was more watchful. Their differences even showed up in which parent they felt the most bonded to. Esau felt more connection with their dad, and Jacob felt more connected to their mom.

There came a day when Esau returned home from working outside and was exhausted. Jacob had been cooking up some stew that day, and Esau was ready for a heaping bowl of it. Scripture says,

> And Esau said to Jacob, "Let me eat some of that red stew, for I am exhausted!" . . . Jacob said, "Sell me your birthright now." Esau said, "I am about to die; of what use is a birthright to me?" Jacob said, "Swear to me now." So he swore to him and sold his birthright to Jacob. Then Jacob gave Esau bread and lentil stew, and he ate and drank and rose and went his way. (Genesis 25:30–34)

Well, that escalated quickly. Your inheritance for a bowl of stew?

Maybe Esau thought it was just a blip on the radar, a throw-away statement made to diffuse his fatigue and appetite. Maybe he didn't think Jacob was serious. Many years went by, and the consequences of his irrational trade-down weren't evident. Life continued as normal.

But the day came when Esau's dad, Isaac, had lived a full life and got ready to give his blessing to Esau, which included declaring Esau's inheritance. Because Esau was the older son, in that culture, he was the one on deck to receive the largest portion of his father's possessions and position. His younger twin, Jacob, would receive a smaller amount. When Rebekah, Jacob and Esau's mom, realized Isaac was going to bless Esau with the inheritance of the firstborn son, she came up with a plan to make sure that Jacob would get the bigger inheritance instead of Esau. Isaac's eyesight wasn't what it used to be, and when Esau went out to go hunting for his father's favorite food, Rebekah and Jacob went into action.

> Rebekah said to her son Jacob, "I heard your father speak to your brother Esau, 'Bring me game and prepare for me delicious food, that I may eat it and bless you before the LORD before I die.' Now therefore, my son, obey my voice as I command you. Go to the flock and bring me two good young goats, so that I may prepare from them delicious food for your father, such as he loves. And you shall bring it to your father to eat, so that he may bless you before he dies." But Jacob said to Rebekah his mother, "Behold, my brother Esau is a hairy man, and I am a smooth man. Perhaps my father will feel me, and I shall seem to be mocking him and bring a curse upon myself and not a blessing." His mother said to him, "Let your curse be on me, my son; only obey my voice, and go, bring them to me."
>
> So he went and took them and brought them to his mother, and his mother prepared delicious food, such as his father loved. Then Rebekah took the best garments of Esau her older son, which were with her in the house, and put them on Jacob her younger son. And the skins of the young goats she put on his hands and on the smooth part of his neck. And she put the delicious food and the bread, which she had prepared, into the hand of her son Jacob. (Genesis 27:6–17)

What came next was a master class in deception. Jacob went to his father with the platter of food and wearing the skins of the young goats. It worked. Isaac blessed Jacob with the bigger blessing, believing he was blessing his firstborn son, Esau.

By the time Esau returned from a hunting trip he'd made to get meat for his dad, his inheritance had been given to Jacob.

The result? Esau was furious. Jacob gained a reputation for being something of a con artist (well deserved). And their relationship, for many years to come, was one filled with anger, suspicion, fear, bitterness, and resentment.

All from trading down.

Now, make no mistake, Jacob and his mom for sure did an endaround to gain the bigger blessing for the younger twin. But Esau was the one who put the whole thing in play when he traded down his rightful inheritance, when he allowed the value of his birthright to be traded for a bowl of bean soup.

Esau did it because he was tired and hungry. And in a moment, he lost everything. He chose a bowl of soup over an inheritance and a blessing. His life was never the same.

I've done the same thing. Not because I was hungry for food, but because I was starving for approval. I have done it to protect a carefully crafted image. I've done it to keep people at arm's length so they wouldn't be able to see my flaws and rough edges.

I've long been willing to trade true relationships for something more surface level. I've traded joy for instant approval. I've traded down, exchanging genuine peace for avoiding conflict.

All that trading down adds up, and not in a positive way.

———

Trading down can show up in a lot of ways. Here's one I've wrestled with: keeping quiet when I should have spoken up. Have you ever been around someone who is manipulative or is a bully? The kind of person who wants to control the room, put everyone in their place, and always get their own way, making harmful comments that are disguised as humor? Yeah, that kind of person. What have I usually done in the presence of someone like that?

Sigh.

I hate to say it, but I've usually kept my mouth shut. I didn't want to risk their wrath. I didn't want their hostile attention turned on me. You might look at that situation and not see where the trading down is. After all, when I didn't speak up, I also didn't have to deal with the aftermath of confronting that unpredictable person.

But it means someone else, somewhere down the line, did. Because I was more interested in protecting myself, it means other people were left in harm's way. I traded down for a moment of temporary comfort instead of the greatness of serving the vulnerable and hurting around me.

That's the selfish part of people pleasing. We get so focused on self-preservation that we forget what true love and friendship are supposed to look like.

Jesus said, "This is my commandment, that you love one another as I have loved you. Greater love has no one than this, that someone lay down his life for his friends. You are my friends if you do what I command you" (John 15:12–14).

Jesus wants me to move past my own discomfort to love others well, even when I'm nervous to confront, when I'm scared to speak up. When I move past my own people pleasing, it means I can be free to help others, to protect those who need protecting.

Here's another of the many ways we can allow our people pleasing to trade down in our lives. Let's say you're always thinking about what others think of you. It's almost like you can hear a dialogue in your head, imagining what they're saying, what they think of your outfit and your car and your boyfriend and your job. You've got a script all mapped out, and you will do anything—anything—to stay in their imagined good graces. You are perceived the way you want to be perceived, with no warts or faults.

But that requires a significant trade-down. To keep up the facade, you can't let anyone get too close. You cut people off in your life when the relationship threatens to go deeper. You can't let anyone see your weaknesses and vulnerabilities. You keep things on a surface level, only showing your accomplishments and glossy

We get so focused on self-preservation that we forget what true love and friendship are supposed to look like.

veneer. You might feel like you're at the height of your carefully crafted image. But the reality is, you've traded down. You've traded genuine relationships that could bless you and help you grow for relationships that keep you in isolation and loneliness. You've traded down from the true freedom of being known and loved for a consuming cage that requires exhausting upkeep.

We've talked a little about that secret ingredient of people pleasing known as selfishness. Does that word surprise you, this idea that your efforts are selfish? I know that can sting a bit . . . or a lot. I've had to deal with that truth myself. The reason our people pleasing is selfish is because it always keeps us at the top of our minds. I know, I know, it can feel like people pleasing is all about trying to buffer and manage all the opinions and perceptions around you. But the deal is, all that mental work has, at its core, the focus on you.

When I'm in an unhealthy people-pleasing mode, I'm always in my mind. I get tunnel vision about what I'm feeling. My nervousness. My anxiety. My desire for comfort. And when my focus is primarily on me and when your focus is primarily on you, we miss all the ways we can authentically engage in the community we were created for, where we serve others from a pure heart and receive the blessing of being part of the family of God.

Esau might not have been people pleasing, but he certainly had tunnel vision. He was really famished and tired. And he was so focused on his own needs and scrambling for what he wanted *in that moment* that he lost sight of the bigger picture. Let's give the cook, Jacob, the benefit of the doubt and say that the stew was delicious, that it satisfied Esau's hunger in that moment. But what about the long term? That stew was only for that fleeting moment. But because Esau allowed it to be hinged to his inheritance, it came at great cost.

It's not lost on me that trading down is attached to our inability and unwillingness to see further than our current feeling, blind to the bigger picture. My husband likes to say that this is the DNA of all sin. Isaac was tricked by Rebekah and Jacob in their costume con because of his physical blindness; Esau tricked himself and traded down because of his spiritual blindness, because of his unwilling-ness to look beyond his immediate state. He lost his inheritance, his relationship with his brother, his family life with his parents. That one hungry, blind moment became his biggest regret.

I had plenty of stew-swapping moments in my early marriage, in those days when we were living in Laredo. I look back on my time in Laredo fondly, but with regret. Not because I didn't get what I wanted but because I selfishly held back. I got so consumed with what everyone thought about me that I felt captive to the bondage of fear and insecurity. To this day, I love my friends there. But I'm also so aware of how much more I could have done to deepen those relationships, to have enjoyed those friendships instead of being focused on my own fears. We could have been more connected, and I could have more freely poured myself into their lives.

Thankfully, God is a God of patience and do-overs. Just because we've gotten it wrong in the past doesn't mean that we can't try again. The story of Jonah in the Bible reminds me of that. God told Jonah to go to the city of Nineveh to warn the people there that they needed to stop living their lives built on sin, to confront them. Seems like a pretty straightforward assignment, right? But Jonah traded down from the bigger vision of being an agent of God's mercy for the people of Nineveh. Instead he decided he'd rather avoid the whole uncomfortable situation. So instead of making his way toward Nineveh, he headed in a different direction, hopping a ship for Tarshish, which was about as far away as he could get.

Jonah was hitchhiking-shiphiking his way 180 degrees in the other direction from where he was supposed to be heading. As it turns out, God had a GPS on Jonah's position the whole time, and He gave Jonah one of the most epic do-overs in history. A huge storm blew up, and the boat was in danger of going down. The sailors were trying to figure out what to do and who might have brought this growing catastrophe upon them. Jonah owned up to the fact that he was likely the cause.

He said to them,

> "Pick me up and hurl me into the sea; then the sea will quiet down for you, for I know it is because of me that this great tempest has come upon you." Nevertheless, the men rowed hard to get back to dry land, but they could not, for the sea grew more and more tempestuous against them. Therefore they called out to the Lord, "O LORD, let us not perish for this man's life, and lay not on us innocent blood, for you, O LORD, have done as it pleased you." So they picked up Jonah and hurled him into the sea, and the sea ceased from its raging. Then the men feared the LORD exceedingly, and they offered a sacrifice to the LORD and made vows. And the Lord appointed a great fish to swallow up Jonah. And Jonah was in the belly of the fish three days and three nights. (Jonah 1:12–17)

God gave Jonah a little timeout in the belly of a fish to reconsider the trade-down he was attempting. God also had that great fish swim its way right up to the beach at Nineveh and spit Jonah up on the shore.

Jonah ended up putting his people pleasing on hold and had a frank and difficult conversation with the people of Nineveh. They were so affected that they turned from their evil ways and God responded with incredible mercy.

———

That's the temptation I felt when my friend asked to talk; to run in the opposite direction. Not because of anything in my friend who needed a listening ear, but because of my own insecurity and fear. I heard the raspy whispers of self-protection and isolation echoing in my head. But I'd also experienced the isolation and trouble that comes when I try to selfishly hide. I knew there were opportunities I had missed in my people pleasing, opportunities I wouldn't have again with certain people, to love and serve them well. And so, on that Tuesday, by God's grace, I chose not to give in.

"Hey, why don't you come over for a bit?" I responded.

I'll be honest, I had to crush my pride as she entered my toy-littered living room. I had to get over the fact that we could have this time together and that I might not have some amazing, super spiritual, revolutionary thing to say to her that would fix everything. But when she came through the door, I was able to take my focus off myself and focus on her. While her problems were big, what she needed that day was simple. She needed a friend. She needed someone to talk to. We sat on the couch for hours while my girls played and our coffee cooled. There were times we laughed. There were times we cried. We talked about some of the most painful aspects of what she was going through.

Did I have the magic pill of advice that solved all of it for her? Nope. And that really wasn't even the point. Simply by my being available and vulnerable, God allowed me to stand outside of my people pleasing for something better.

It was a wonderful time, and I realized something remarkable. As she headed out the door, I told her, "Anytime you want to talk, come on over." And I meant it. It hit me that I felt refreshed by the time we'd had together. I felt blessed to have been entrusted with her story and to be able to be there for her. Even more fascinating was that I felt comforted. The things I'd been trying to protect myself from, the chance that I would be drained, that I would be judged? As it turns out, to be in the presence of someone who is open and honest about their challenges and failures and circumstances makes you feel not as alone, lets you be seen as well. My original hesitation, my fears that I wouldn't measure up, all seemed pretty insignificant and silly at the end of that day.

Simply by my being available and vulnerable, God allowed me to stand outside of my people pleasing for something better.

Huh. Who knew?

God. When we stop making trades from our fears, He provides what we need to love others well.

———

Here's something I've come to realize about people pleasing: everybody deals with an element of it. As humans, as people created for connection, unhealthy people pleasing comes for us and body slams us to the mat at times, making us think we need to make trades that we never would, if we were in a fulfilled, healthy, spiritually satisfied place.

But just like we can get the things God has intended for us as good twisted up, like needing other people in our lives, it can happen with fear. The Bible tells us to fear God—a right and holy fear, a reverential awe and love for Him. It's because of the combination of both His all-powerful nature and His grace He gives us through Jesus. The right fear of God is because He is in control of everything, and, at the same time, kind, compassionate, and loving. To have a fear of the Lord is to trust Him, to believe His Word, to know that He will do what He has promised.

That place reserved in our hearts for a reverential fear of God can get traded down for a fear of man. What do I mean by the phrase *fear of man*? It means to make your concern about others' opinions, reactions, judgments, and responses bigger than anything else, even bigger than God.

A distorted form of people pleasing is another way of saying a *fear of man*.

King Solomon, considered in the Bible to be one of the wisest of men, had this to say about it: "The fear of man lays a snare, but whoever trusts in the LORD is safe" (Proverbs 29:25).

I see with a growing conviction that I've often operated out of a fear of man that has to do with others, but I also see that fear-of-man focus also includes me operating out of pleasing myself. Does that make sense? In my people pleasing, I have elevated my own fears about protecting myself above my reverential fear of God. And that, my friend, is sin, through and through.

We are so consumed with others' approval and recognition and acceptance that we become enslaved to it. This fear of man is crippling. It shows up in the ways I've described in my life. But for you, it could show up in so many other ways. Sometimes it looks like oversocializing. Overstretching. For me, it's more of an isolation. Clinging to the strand of approval I may have and being too afraid to mess it up if I interact too much, too often.

Regardless of how it shows up, it's crippling. It's a bondage that comes with a lot of regret.

———

In terms of a cautionary tale, it's important to see what happened to Esau post-stew trade-down. As you've already learned, he lost his inheritance. When Esau realized what had happened, he begged his father, "'Have you not reserved a blessing for me?' Isaac answered and said to Esau, 'Behold, I have made him lord over you, and all his brothers I have given to him for servants, and with grain and wine I have sustained him. What then can I do for you, my son?' Esau said to his father, 'Have you but one blessing, my father? Bless me, even me also, O my father.' And Esau lifted up his voice and wept" (Genesis 27:36–38).

He also lost his relationship with his twin. He was so enraged with his brother's deception that he plotted to kill him. Jacob fled to his uncle's house to escape Esau's plans. For years they were estranged, and Esau had to live with the knowledge that the future he should have had was squandered in a moment of temporary hunger.

We encounter Esau again when the writer of the book of

We are so consumed with others' approval and recognition and acceptance that we become enslaved to it.

Hebrews, in the New Testament, gives us this insight about the rest of Esau's life after trading down. Hebrews 12:15–17 says,

> See to it that no one fails to obtain the grace of God; that no "root of bitterness" springs up and causes trouble, and by it many become defiled; that no one is sexually immoral or unholy like Esau, who sold his birthright for a single meal. For you know that afterward, when he desired to inherit the blessing, he was rejected, for he found no chance to repent, though he sought it with tears.

Friend, I don't want to cry Esau's tears of regret. I don't want you to weep that way, realizing too late what you've traded down for, what you've left behind in your efforts to insulate and protect yourself. I'm tired of trading down, of trading something good and lasting and refreshing for some form of temporal, cheap self-preservation. I'm guessing you are too.

There is a path forward! It's freeing and liberating. You can take that path the next time you find yourself hungry for approval, facing the temptation to forgo the best for the short term. That's where we're headed, you and me, as we continue to move forward.

Let's Chat About It

Sometimes the cage of people pleasing looks like a measly bowl of stew. Sometimes it looks like a ship heading in the other direction. Sometimes it looks like sitting in the belly of a big fish, sorting through your own selfishness.

1. When have you found yourself trapped by your own people pleasing?
2. Think about a time when you let a selfish form of people pleasing keep you from a longer-term blessing. What were you trying to avoid? What were you trying to satisfy?
3. What stands out most to you in the stories of Esau and Jonah?

Read again the key verse shared in this chapter: "The fear of man lays a snare, but whoever trusts in the LORD is safe" (Proverbs 29:25). Take a moment to pray for God's help and guidance as we continue our journey together. Ask Him to show you where you've traded down in the past, missing His best for you in exchange for temporary comfort. Thank Him that you have the opportunity to learn and to move forward. Confess to Him where you have allowed the selfish motives of people pleasing to keep you from loving others well. He is a God of mercy, of grace, and He delights when His children come to Him.

Chapter 6

THE CRITICS

SHOULD YOU EVER FIND YOURSELF ON A REALITY television show showcasing your growing-up years, here's one thing I can tell you for sure that you never, ever want to show in a post on social media once you become an adult and have kids of your own:

Car seats.

When we had our kids, did Jeremy and I make sure their car seats were correctly installed? Absolutely. Did we consult with the professionals? You bet. Did the hospital even double-check to make sure we had the right equipment to strap our babies into before we made the trek home? Correct.

In every way, shape, and form that we could, we made sure we were on top of all the car seat safety standards and protocols.

But any time someone sees a glimpse of our car seats in a social media post, they've got some opinions for us. It happens all the time to my sisters as well. We'll get comments about how our kids' car seats aren't installed properly or aren't the best type of car seats or that the straps are too tight or they're too loose or the angle isn't right or any other comment you can imagine. Seriously, the car seat thing is a whole hot topic, sweating controversy from its pores.

And the funny thing is that all those comments contradict each other and say different things and are all presented with the utmost confidence. People claiming to be experts of all stripes when it comes to car seats disagree with each other *right there in the comments*, give opposing opinions, and say that their approach is the right approach.

(Another hot topic? Our kids' hair. If it's not parted perfectly straight. If their curls seem the least bit tangled. People lose their minds. A small civil war breaks out in the comments section. Every. Time.)

I can only imagine if I tried to follow each piece of advice. Our car seats would be up, down, sideways, and all other kinds of directions, and I know there would still be people out there who would find fault. We choose to listen to the professionals in our kids' lives, stay on top of pediatric recommendations and updates, and leave the rest of the noise behind. It's the only way to not stay stuck in a quicksand of indecision and confusion. And indecision and confusion wouldn't keep our kids safe.

When Jeremy and I got married, we made a pact with each other that we wouldn't read all the headlines about us. As best as we could, we wanted to keep a healthy and *real* perspective on who we really are, not influenced by either the hype or the hostility of the media. For the most part, we've kept to that approach. Sometimes we have to check in, both because of the work we do and to protect our family. But I knew from growing up Duggar that you can be praised, loved, adored, and puffed up by fans or absolutely dragged and destroyed by your haters. Trying to keep up with all the roller coasters of that is a great way to keep your head and heart in a constant spin. And then there's the whole flattery aspect that comes with some notoriety. If you took it too seriously, all that sweet talk could go right to your head.

Here's the deal in all of it: flattery goes right to your head, and criticism cuts to your heart.

And the same people in your DMs will do both to you.

As good a job as Jeremy and I have done to create boundaries and emotional resilience to the opinions of strangers on the internet, I have to tell you, it still makes an impact. I call it the outside critic, the feedback of faultfinders and frenemies that is the fuel to my people-pleasing fears.

But there's another kind of critic in my life.

I have an *inside* critic that can get stirred up, either by an outside critic moment or all on my own. It goes a little something like this: I'll finish, say, a project, something I've worked hard on and put a lot of thought and counsel into, but then along will come my own band of voices, blowing up my own internal comment section:

Couldn't you have just put in a little more effort? Are you sure this is your best?

There are other people out there who could have done that better. Why do you even try?

That was a really stupid thing to say. You shouldn't say anything next time.

No, as a homeschooler I didn't experience the kind of schoolgirl bullying growing up that you might have, but boy, have I been bullied.

By me.

It's so wild to think that as intentional as I've been to protect myself and my family from the judgment of the online world, I keep letting *me* create unfair hype internally about *me*.

And there is nothing that will get your inside critic stirred up like deciding to write a book on people pleasing. *Who do you think you are, trying to help people with their people pleasing?*

You're not an expert! You still have so far to go! What are you thinking?

Being raised in the religious system I was, there was a whole lot of hyperanalyzing of one's own behavior, held up against the most intense standard. While I get what got me here in terms of my inside critic, there are still times it's the loudest and most familiar voice in my head. After all, I've been listening to it for a long time.

Just the other day at church, Jeremy was across the courtyard talking with a friend. I walked over to chat with them. It was super chill, friendly, laid-back. I made a statement about something during the conversation, just taking part in the talk. But for hours afterward, *bam!* That voice came barreling in. I dissected every syllable I'd said. I replayed it over and over. All I could hear in my head was, *That was stupid. That was really stupid.* I felt like an idiot for the rest of the day. Had Jeremy or his friend made me feel that way? No. Was there an eye roll or a snicker from either of them as I chatted? Absolutely not. But it wasn't just the three of us standing there talking. It was Jer, his friend, me . . . and my inside critic, thumbs flying over an internal keyboard, tearing me up in the comments.

Believe me, there are days when, if I could block myself from commenting about myself, I would.

I have a feeling you know exactly what I'm talking about. When you're a people pleaser, your internal comments section is usually busting at the seams with contradictory, confusing commentary about who you are and how you show up in the world. And all those comments are written and submitted by you.

There's a relationship between the outside critics and the inside critic in my life, one that I've only recently begun to understand fully. As much as we're careful not to buy into the hype about us on media or in our socials, those outside critical voices still break through. And when the voices of outside critics start to hit my airways, my inside critic stirs to life. Those things the outside critics are saying either confirm something negative I've been thinking about myself or make me aware of a new place to pick on myself.

Here's what I've learned about the relationship between the outside critics in my life and the inner critic I carry around with me. One feeds the other. When someone says something hurtful or rude to me, my inner critic loves to pick that thing up and chew on it a while, creating even more commentary about where I come up short. And when my inner critic has been busy saying all kinds of judgy things to me, I often find connections in what I'm saying to myself in the words of others.

Where do your outside critics usually come from? It might be that mom in your children's playgroup who always seems to hit a nerve with what she says about parenting. Maybe it's someone at work who can't ever seem to simply tell you you've done a good job, but always has "feedback" with subtle jabs. It may be a cruel comment on social media or a whisper of slander being spread about you. Wherever you're encountering that outside critic, your inner critic can pop up like it's feeding time at the zoo, gulping down the commentary. There will be outside critics in your world, people you work with, neighbors, those you go to church with, and, yes, maybe even those who live in the same house. They can activate your inside critic to start throwing rocks at your fragile heart, splintering and shattering you.

You're probably familiar with the phrase "glass houses." Best I can tell, it comes from a quote from fourteenth-century writer Geoffrey Chaucer. He wrote, "Whose house is of glass must not throw stones." What he meant is that we all have our fragile places and our faults. If we start throwing rocks at others, we're likely going to smash not only them but ourselves as well. You and I, we live in glass houses today. The glass of the screens and the devices we're always on bring the idea of living in glass houses to a whole new level. Like never before, our lives are on display all the time. We present ourselves online. We interact with people across the globe on a regular basis.

We travel to other cities and countries, and we meet more people along the way. There's a statistic out there that says you and I will meet eighty thousand people in our lifetimes.[1] That's a huge jump from the number of people we would have met if we lived, say, a hundred or a thousand years ago.

We're all peering at each other, all the time, through the walls of our glass houses. We're sizing each other up, checking out each other's outfits and kitchens, gauging what having it together looks like. We hide more of our faults in the cabinets, and we put out a buffet of perfection. We even do it when we're posting #relatable stuff, trying to stay on that razor's edge of *perfect* but also *just like you.* And more than we're wondering where so-and-so got that great couch in her home redecorating post, as people pleasers, we're silently asking, *How do I measure up? What does everyone think when they look at me?*

When you're already your own worst critic, this level of exposure only raises the volume on that critical voice. You and I can spend all day long looking at the carefully curated feeds of other women in our ages and stages of life who seem to have it more together and more figured out. And then we slide into our own DMs with all kinds of harsh statements about how we just aren't measuring up.

I can turn off the outside critics.

Random person online? I'll get over it.

My friends? Okay, that stirs me up.

But me? I can't turn me off.

I can be ruthless to myself over silly things. A line I often repeat to Jer when I'm getting ready for the day is, "Does this look stupid?" Or after I've left a conversation, "Did I say something stupid?" I can be so harsh and cruel . . . to myself. I am sometimes Siskel and sometimes Ebert.

But this translates to significant spiritual issues too. I can condemn myself because I didn't read my Bible that morning or I didn't pray long enough or I got distracted during a sermon. And my whole relationship with Jesus comes crashing in. I start to spiral in my mind, thinking, *You're this or that*, any number of ways to condemn myself.

Trust me, whatever you think of me, I've thought of myself. And worse.

It reminds me of a story in the Bible where Jesus took on this very thing.

———

Jesus had His own way of talking about glass houses. One day, He saw a group of religious leaders getting ready to punish a woman they accused of sleeping around, and the punishment of the time was to stone her, meaning that they literally picked up rocks to throw at her until she died. As the religious leaders were getting ready to carry out their sentence against her, they brought her to Jesus. They used it as an opportunity to try to start a debate. They hoped to catch Jesus going against the law. They asked him, "'Teacher, this woman has been caught in the act of adultery. Now in the Law, Moses commanded us to stone such women. So what do you say?' This they said to test him, that they might have some charge to bring against him" (John 8:4–6).

Jesus didn't fall for it. Instead, He stooped down and began writing in the dirt with His finger. There are plenty of opinions about what He was drawing. Was it a list of the sins of the religious leaders? Was it a symbol or a picture? Scripture doesn't say, but it's what Jesus says next that is so compelling.

"Let him who is without sin among you be the first to throw a stone at her" (John 8:7).

When Jesus looked up again from His canvas of dust, all the religious leaders had dropped their rocks and left. Not a stone had been thrown at the accused woman. Why? I think it's because these guys got the point. They knew they had their own sins, things that could warrant them being at the receiving end of a rock-throwing jury.

But here's something that can be easy to miss in the story. After the accusers left, the woman was left standing there as Jesus continued to write in the sand. The Bible says, "Jesus stood up and said to her, 'Woman, where are they? Has no one condemned you?' She said, 'No one, Lord.' And Jesus said, 'Neither do I condemn you; go, and from now on sin no more'" (John 8:10–11).

Did you catch it?

Jesus told her that He didn't condemn her. Technically, He had every right to. In her adultery, she had broken the law, and the law at that time meant that adultery was a capital offense. She should have died for her sin. It's important to point this out because I think we could gloss over this story, making light of her offense. It was a big deal, with a big penalty. Jesus didn't condemn her because He ultimately took her punishment upon Himself. Now, if her accusers couldn't condemn her because they had their own issues, and if Jesus didn't condemn her, did she have any business condemning herself?

You probably noticed that there's a word that comes up a lot in the previous paragraph. It's that word *condemn*, and it means "to give judgment against, to judge worthy of punishment."[2] It's a word we don't like much in our culture. It's what we hear when we watch a courtroom drama, when the defendant is "condemned" to their punishment after being found guilty. It's the word we think of when someone is judging us. It's a word that can make us uncomfortable because it's so tied to punishment, loss, and failure.

My inside critic was always condemning me, passing all kinds of judgment against me. And that was how I treated myself for a long, long time. Frankly, from the religious system I was part of as a child, I was trained to do it. It's like I was willing to punish myself ahead of time so that no one else would have to. Somehow the math in my head was that if I beat myself up enough, maybe, just maybe, I could avoid any commentary from the outside critics in my life. I'd come up with harsh disciplines to run my life by. I'd get up earlier than everyone. I'd try to pray longer. I'd feel guilty if I felt good. If I was having a good hair day and liked what I saw in the mirror, then I'd beat myself up about that. I was so consumed with living in my glass house, and so worried someone would throw a stone, that I was hurling boulders at myself all the time as a preventive measure.

Which makes no sense, not when I say it now. But that's how I lived for far too long. And when I'm not careful, I go there again.

Jesus showed that to this young woman who *did* deserve to die under Israelite law. She was supposed to be stoned. But Jesus gave her a way out: Him. He is the answer. He can forgive your sin because He takes the punishment for you. Jesus was not shoving her sin under the rug. He was showing her that He would be stoned instead of her. Why? So she could live in freedom from her sin—from being condemned and being controlled. She could walk in freedom because of Jesus.

So can I. And so can you.

I want to make sure that you know that there is a side of that word *condemn* that is for our good. It shows me the comparison of what I deserve for my actions versus what Jesus has done for me. See, my sins and yours, they *should* lead to us being condemned, to us having to suffer the full consequences of our behavior. Our sins and shortcomings may be different, but just like the woman caught in adultery, you and I face disastrous results because of where we mess up.

When we really get our heads and hearts around seeing what we deserve for our choices, when we are honest about what we should be condemned for, we can begin to see and appreciate what Jesus does for us—that He forgives what we've done. It's a "right" kind of condemning because it leads me to get honest about the price of my behavior, and it fills me with gratitude for the salvation Jesus gives me.

Here's where I have to be careful. When I realize where I've messed up, I can let the wrong kind of condemnation take me into a selfish spiral of self-focus. It's that inside critic again, the one that doesn't offer me hope, the one that puts all my worth in my performance. The "right" kind of conviction and condemnation helps me remember that because of Jesus, I'm forgiven. I get a fresh start. I get to try again. I get to grow. My inside critic and my outside critics don't shame me into life-giving change. Grace leads me into change.

And then Jesus reminds me, "I don't condemn you." Not because it's okay to sin but because He took the punishment I deserve.

———

While we were living in Laredo, we visited a local restaurant, and I found an unexpected ingredient in my meal. I'd ordered the stuffed mushrooms, a dish that has a great combo of savory and hearty, the delicious gooiness of melted cheese with a nice crunch of toasted, buttery breadcrumbs on top. But this particular night, there was a sparkle that wasn't supposed to be there.

There was glass in my food.

Now, it would be reasonable to call over the server and let them know, right? But the people-pleasing approach is not to make a fuss, not to say anything, just to chew glass. Literally, in this case. (Thankfully, Jeremy intervened, and we let the restaurant know. In the doing, we likely saved another customer from chewing glass as well. But I was more worried about making a fuss than fixing the problem.)

From chewing glass to breaking glass houses, my people pleasing has left me damaged. And when you hurl a rock through a window to your soul, like I've often done as my own worst critic, you do damage to the beautiful things that could be growing in your life.

Have you noticed what's at the core of all that critical contribution, whether it's coming from inside our own glass houses or we feel like we're getting rocks thrown at us?

It's judging.

It's making judgment calls about someone else's life or your own, with a focus on faultfinding and finger-pointing.

Over time, I began to realize that I wasn't just dealing with a harsh inside critic who was only critiquing me. I was silently doing it to others around me. It had been modeled for me in the religious system in which I was raised, a judging attitude that left no one safe, not me from myself, not from how I evaluated the behavior of others.

It's one of the weird parts of being your own worst critic; it feels like you're only being hard on yourself, but your judging colors everything you see. No matter your conclusion, you're also evaluating other people's worth based on their behaviors. For a long time, I didn't think I was operating out of a judgmental spirit toward others. The voice in my head that was constantly on blast, making a tally of all the places I was messing up, tended to block out anything else.

But over time, I began to realize that I was basing all those criticisms on *something*. Often it was a judgment call I made about someone else's spiritual life. If I were only as spiritual as so-and-so, then I'd read my Bible more; I'd pray more. Sometimes it was a judgment call about someone else's physical appearance. If I could just drop a few pounds, maybe I could get closer to looking like so-and-so.

Do you see the problem?

I was judging, evaluating, deciding the worth of each of those people based on something that was really none of my business, then using that judgment to set a scale of expectations for myself, then beating myself up when I couldn't meet it. Yes, I recognize that we usually think of judgment as thinking negatively about someone. But I've come to see that in my "positive" judging of who I thought was more spiritual, more self-disciplined, more *more*, I was also making judgment calls about who I *didn't* see as role-model worthy. Ugh.

Judging can show up when you don't even know you're doing it. Before Jeremy and I became parents, we had lots of ideas about parenting. We'd encounter a family who, say, had their kids on a really strict bedtime schedule, and we'd think, *We're not doing that. We're rolling with it when we have kids. We're gonna be laid-back and we're going to still have fun in the evenings and be social.*

And then we had kids. And we had kids who handle life a whole lot better when they get to bed around the same time every night. And yes, it cut into our social schedule. And yes, it's not exactly convenient. And yes, we totally understand when people who aren't yet parents want to roll their eyes around us when we head out at 6:30 in the evening to go back to the house to start the whole bedtime routine. And we know families who ended up with kids who flourish and operate just fine on a day-by-day, night-by-night improv routine.

We have to look at each other and just laugh, thinking back to our inexperienced critic selves who thought we had it all figured out before we were even in the parenting room. As Jeremy likes to say, the famous film critics Siskel and Ebert never made a film but made a career out of criticizing something they themselves could never make. And we all listened to them for cinematic advice. Sometimes you're throwing rocks at a glass house you haven't even inhabited yet, as if you could even possibly understand the challenges and choices of those who are living in the middle of it.

I've seen it several times, and maybe you have too. There will be that person who is so harsh about a certain topic in life, something they see other people doing that they just go nuclear on. They've got a lot to say about it. It becomes something of their "brand," that subject they just can't seem to let go of and they discuss without any show of concern, compassion, or mercy. And then comes the day when the very thing they've been pointing out in others is revealed to be a major issue in their own life.

We have a tendency as humans to really home in on something

we ourselves struggle with, but we call it out in others in a loud voice, trying to distance ourselves from the issue in our own hearts and lives. Take, for example, people who choose to go into someone's messages on social media and shred them over their physical appearance. (I've been on the receiving end of this experience, with all kinds of comments about the bags under my eyes, my current state of complexion, that I'm too fluffy, too skinny, too whatever. It's a great way *not* to start a Monday morning.)

Let's unwind that a bit. Why? Why does someone need to critique someone else's physical appearance? What I'm learning more and more is that the person who feels compelled to comment is likely also beating themselves up about their own appearance. That critic stream seems to flow both ways at all times. Even if it's not voiced in a format like commenting on someone's social post, that critic track runs backward and forward all the time, sometimes commenting on someone else, sometimes commenting personally.

Given that you and I deal with our own worst critics being right between our own ears, you might think that I'm going to go on telling you that you should never take a hard look at yourself, that you should never have a tough thing to say to you, that you should only treat your heart and your motives with velvet gloves.

Well, no. I'm not going to tell you that. Because if we want freedom, true freedom, we're going to have to get radically honest with ourselves *about* ourselves.

Let's go back to the story we were looking at earlier, about the woman who was caught in adultery and brought to Jesus. We looked at verse 11 in John 8, where Jesus told the woman He didn't condemn her. But that's not all He said, remember? After He told her that He didn't condemn her, He said these eight important words: "Go, and from now on sin no more."

People don't like to talk about sin these days. Use the word *sin* to describe a behavior and you'll likely stir up the idea that you're judging someone. But I want you to consider something that might feel pretty revolutionary: it is possible to look at our sin and do it in such a way that we're not condemning. That's why the example of Jesus in John 8 is such an important one. Jesus clearly told the woman He was not condemning her, and He clearly told her to leave her life of sin. Right there together, in a back-to-back moment, He extended her both grace and—get ready for it—freedom.

Yep.

Facing the sin in our life and experiencing the forgiveness and change that comes from encountering Jesus is *freedom*.

I wanted to be careful when working on this topic because it's tender, this balance between overcoming our inside critic while also leaving room for healthy conviction about behaviors that are hurting us, places where sin has a hold on us. Sometimes when we discover something that's been holding us back, like an inside critic or an outside critic, we can overcompensate in our desire to overcome those voices. If you were raised in a rigid religious system or a highly critical home and it felt like *everything* was a sin, and that everyone was commenting on your behavior, it can be hard to readjust. Just like I've done by isolating myself as a result of my style of people pleasing, we can go too far, not allowing anyone to speak into our lives, not willing to face our own issues and sins.

When we do this, we set ourselves up for a big fall.

The reality is, I've been way too hard on myself for things that didn't really matter. And, sometimes, I've been too easy on myself for things that did. That's the tricky part with being ruthlessly honest about yourself, about your motives, but without hopeless condemnation; it's tough to get it just right, to keep your internal settings at that place between oversensitive and totally jaded.

———

I love the beach, and I'm so glad that we can take our girls to the beach here in California now, not too far of a drive from our house.

There's just something about the salty water and the warm sand that's good for my soul. When Jeremy and I were living in Texas, we were about two and a half hours from the Texas coast, but we didn't make it over there for any beach days. I did, however, go with a friend to an appointment in Corpus Christi, which is on the coast, and I noticed something interesting there. Texas coastal houses have a feature that California coastal houses don't. When you first see a Texas coastal house, you might notice that there seems to be a heavy metal bar above each window and above the doors. Those metal bars don't look all that decorative, and I wasn't sure what they were the first time I saw them.

It turns out, inside those metal bars is a really important piece of equipment for Texas beach living. They are the casing for hurricane shutters; when a hurricane enters the Gulf Coast, you can lower the shutters housed in those metal casings above your windows and doors. The hurricane shutters seal up your house to keep the storm-brewed elements out. When those Texas coast houses lower their hurricane shutters, it makes the neighborhoods look like every house has put on armor. It's a pretty surreal-looking environment, something out of an apocalyptic movie. In California, houses don't usually have hurricane shutters like that because there simply aren't hurricanes here. But living on the beaches of the unpredictable Gulf Coast, many Texas houses do.

That's what I think we can have a tendency to do when we feel like we've had stones thrown at us, at our glass houses of life. Once we identify what's been going on, how we've let the critics come for us over and over, we can go into hurricane-shutter mode, slamming mental metal over any place that feels fragile. We shut people out, refuse to listen, and pump ourselves up with quotes like *Nobody's gonna talk to me like that!* We sit in the cool dark of our protected house and congratulate ourselves on blocking out the world.

Here's the problem:

We've been talking about glass houses as a symbol of our fragile inner lives, but there's something to consider. A glass house could actually be a greenhouse, designed to bring in light and warmth to create a place where plants can flourish and grow, regardless of the weather outside. The glass isn't a weakness in this glass house. It's the thing that helps create a vibrant and blooming environment.

The funny part about how I've lived in my own glass house is that I was forever trying to pull down hurricane shutters. I didn't want someone to see in, to see the things that are messy in my life. I can pin part of that on having my life on full display from the time I was ten years old on television. Believe me, it gets a little old, feeling like a ton of people are always pressed up against the windows of your heart, hands cupped against the panes, peering in. Just because you grew up in the public eye doesn't mean you have to stay there. You don't have to stay on social media, posting your days to the world. Delete that stuff if it's taking up too much space in your head and heart. Privacy is a needed and good thing. It's okay to need some space.

But the solution for needing some privacy and space is not to block *everyone* out. That's not how God designed us. He created us for community. We're not meant to do life alone, in the dark, trapped behind shutters. You can't experience community without some exposure. We're made for transparency with people; it's what lets the light in. It's how we grow.

The reality is, I need people in my life who can help me see my blind spots, point out what's holding me back, and help me grow. Scripture says, "Iron sharpens iron, and one man sharpens another" (Proverbs 27:17). This means that when we have relationships with others in which we cooperate lovingly in each other's growth, we're both the better for it.

The reality is, I need me to be honest with me. Romans 12:3 says, "By the grace given to me I say to everyone among you not to think of himself more highly than he ought to think, but to think with sober judgment, each according to the measure of faith that God has assigned." We aren't supposed to condemn ourselves, but we are supposed to confront ourselves about sin in our lives.

Am I saying we should just let anyone into the glass house of our hearts? No. We have to be wise about who we are in community with. We have to be wise about who we listen to. And we can listen in a different way, with a different motive, a different filter, if you will.

Look, I still fail. I critique myself and overthink and spend too much time with me on my mind. But now I realize that it's a fresh opportunity to be reminded of God's grace, of my need for Him. When I start to throw stones, at others or at myself, faster and faster these days I'm reminded that it's God who covers my sin, not my efforts, not my finger-pointing, not my hurricane-shutter-slamming ways.

Sometimes I just need to remind myself of that.

That's why I want to remind you. Because the freedom I find when I'm honest about my sins and when I'm gentle with the truth all brings me back to the mystery of the grace of Jesus.

And in that grace, I'm free to put down any rock I've been tempted to throw. Even the ones I'm aiming at myself.

Let's Chat About It

1. How do you talk to yourself? How do you talk about yourself? Does it match how you would talk about your best friend or someone you love? If not, what's the difference?

2. Do you find that you have one set of standards for yourself and another for other people? Describe that.

3. Within our own harshness with ourselves can lie a deeper judgment of others than we may have even realized. Do you think you might be dealing with a condemning and judgmental heart as part of your people-pleasing ways? Where do you think that comes from?

4. It's an important moment to realize that the glass house you've been living in can be a greenhouse, a place of warmth, growth, and transparency. What would you like to "grow" in your life?

Let's think on this verse before we head into the next chapter:

Let no corrupting talk come out of your mouths, but only such as is good for building up, as fits the occasion, that it may give grace to those who hear.
EPHESIANS 4:29

Chapter 7

I CAN'T LET YOU
SEE ME MESS UP

IT WAS THE GROCERY CART RODEO AND, NOT TO BE A plot spoiler, I lost.

Look, it's not like I try to go find clumsy; clumsy just finds me. Gravity and I can be getting along just fine, and then, *wham*, all of a sudden something shifts, and I find myself tripping over air, dropping plates for no reason, and generally stumbling through some of the level sidewalks of life.

Thankfully, a lot of these moments happen when no one but Jeremy is watching. And let me tell you, he finds my clumsiness highly entertaining. He tries to soften it by telling me that I'm adorable, but whatever.

It was an average day at the grocery store, with an average mission; I was picking up supplies for one of my kids' birthdays. I love throwing parties to celebrate my girls, and while Jeremy and I like to keep things pretty simple, we still want them to be special. We had friends coming over to celebrate, and I needed to pick up some extra food and treats and water for the festivities.

I piled my cart with all the things I needed, including an extra flat of water and several bags of ice. I don't completely understand why grocery shopping cart Tetris works the way it does, but just because you can get all that stuff in your cart before you go through the checkout process does not mean it's all going to go back in the same way. After paying and having my cart reloaded, I found myself with the flat of water bottles hanging off the front of the cart and three ten-pound bags of ice in the kid seat, steering my cart into the parking lot with one hand, hanging on to the ice with the other.

I don't have the physics knowledge to describe what happened next. One minute I was casually pushing my cart, making my way to my car. And the next minute, gravity changed course. Somehow, the weight of the water bottles on the front of the cart suddenly became approximately 8,000 percent heavier and the entire cart started tipping forward.

I got this, I thought optimistically, going for a better grip on the ice and trying to pull all four wheels of the cart back to the ground.

Which was quickly followed by the thought, *Oh, I don't got this*.

I'm not the tallest person, and the way the cart was tipping was now lifting me up like a kid on an aggressive carnival ride, up on my tippy toes, frantically trying to maintain contact with the ground. I kicked and twisted, trying to gain some ground. There were some scary split seconds where I thought the cart and I were going down together, but somehow, at the last minute, I got the cart back into position, albeit breaking a serious nervous sweat.

Me at my finest.

I hope no one saw that, I thought to myself. It was embarrassing enough to have witnessed myself in this predicament, much less having some kind of audience.

I got to my car to load the groceries, got everything in, checked my shins for signs of my struggle, and headed home, grateful that I hadn't become a public spectacle in the midst of a perfect example of Jing Clumsy.

Whew.

Except not whew, because days later, there it was, splashed across all the gossip sites. Yep, the paparazzi had caught it all, with multiple photos depicting the whole incident:

"Ex-Reality TV Star Almost Falls in Parking Lot!"

"Jinger Takes a Tumble!"

"A Jam-Packed Cart Almost Creates a Disaster for Jinger!"

"Short-Shorts and Shopping Cart Woes for Former Duggar Star!"

Lovely. Just lovely.

At the end of the day, it ended up being funny to me. I count that as progress, as growth, because there have certainly been times in my life when I would have been completely mortified that this moment was captured and broadcast-blasted for the world to see.

I'm making progress on this people-pleasing thing. One grocery-store-cart roller-coaster ride at a time.

———

I don't know about you, but I don't love messing up in front of people. I've got quite the combo platter going when it comes to this, because in addition to my bless-my-heart people-pleasing ways, I also grew up playing violin and piano, and when you're performing music, it definitely changes the experience if you're constantly hitting the wrong notes or getting lost on where you are in the music. I was also raised with a big group of directors and cameras and producers following me around, and believe me when I say, it was a whole lot easier to help them get the shot right the first time than having to do things over and over and over again when all I wanted to do was go play outside.

Overarching all of this was the religious system I was raised in. It was one that demanded a form of faux Christianity that was built on the appearance of holiness. It was so important to uphold this appearance that many underlying issues, struggles, and sins were pushed far back into the dark, never discussed, and never dealt with, unless it was in a twisted form of "confession" that still never really dealt with the issues. If you messed up in that setting, you were at risk for losing your community by not living up to the Gothard standards.

Then there's the bonus pack I seem to have come with, that pesky side of perfectionism that rides sidecar to my personality: I really, really want to get things right.

Which means I don't want to give you any reason to think I'm a mess.

For a long while, as I mentioned, my solution to this conundrum was to keep people at arm's length. It was the only thing I seemed to be able to come up with. I knew I needed people in my life. I wanted friends. I wanted community. But I also wanted to be safe from any kind of screwup on my part influencing someone's opinion of me.

You might not have realized it if you'd been watching me. It *looked* like I was engaging with people, going to dinner parties, hanging out with friends. I really like people, and I knew there was tremendous value in pursuing friendships. But on the inside? I was being as cautious as a spy trying not to be caught on the wrong side of enemy lines. I watched every word I said. I never disclosed anything about challenges I was having, questions I was facing, sin issues I was dealing with. I kept it all hidden away, too afraid to be transparent with my friends about my struggles.

I didn't want anyone to hear me hit the wrong note, make the mistake, overturn the proverbial apple (I mean, grocery) cart. And the best way to have people in my life but not give them any reason to think less of me was to hide in plain sight.

I have to wonder now if I might have come off as distant or maybe even a little conceited. After all, when someone is hiding right in front of you, their best strategy is to be very, very still and quiet. And that was my strategy. Someone asking for my opinion? Uh, no thank you. A girlfriend at coffee telling me about her challenges in her marriage and asking how I navigated things like that? I'd want to shut down. The risks were way too high to let people in at that level.

Okay, yes, to be fair, growing up on television for sure makes you more cautious than the average bear, and for good reason. There have been all kinds of stories about me through the years, posted on social media, showing up in gossip magazines. I've had very little control over what gets said about me in those public forums. There have also been times I've felt a little burned by someone I thought might become a friend, only to realize they were only interested in a connection to me because they thought it might give them a little "celebrity" status.

That's not unique to me. Maybe you've had situations where a rumor went wild at work or school, where you were judged and judged loudly by people who barely know you. You've been burned by someone you considered a friend, someone who stabbed you in the back. You've been used by people when they want something from you. You've had your times as well when you opened up to someone and they used it against you.

So you and me? We have good reason to be cautious. And there are times when being cautious around others is smart, is a good idea. We shouldn't be vulnerable with just anyone. We can't trust everyone with our deepest places of growth.

But that's not what I'm talking about. I'm talking about closing myself off and only presenting the things I thought I could put forward with some kind of perfection.

There are at least a couple of problems with that approach. Problems like gravity. And grocery carts. And any number of my natural human imperfections. So the odds are completely in favor of the fact that at some point, I'm going to mess up. Plus, when you're constantly trying to keep people at a distance but you also want a relationship with them, there comes a point where those two goals just can't mesh.

This really came to a head early in my marriage with Jeremy. There's nothing like marriage with someone you deeply love to make the seesaw of distance and closeness teeter on the edge. Jeremy would ask my opinion on something, and I'd go along. "Whatever you want, whatever you think," I'd murmur. Yes, part of that was my deep conflict avoidance. But I also didn't want him to think I was dumb. I didn't want Jeremy to think any less of me. So I'd just go along, and, in doing so, I was keeping Jeremy from really knowing me, my preferences, things I might say or do that were kind of silly or dumb, and any other number of things I wanted to keep hidden.

But Jeremy wasn't going to let me get away with it. He knew that we both wanted a true, deep, intimate relationship, not just a polite one. He'd see me get so embarrassed about something I didn't know or some clumsy stunt I'd pull. I'd be so mortified I'd be fighting back tears. "Why are you so embarrassed, babe?" he'd ask me. "It's just you and me. You never have to be shy or ashamed with me. I love you." Over time, I started to believe him, not just in theory but in practice. I started asking questions about things I didn't understand, even at the risk of sounding silly or dumb. I started seeing it as funny when I'd trip over my own two feet. Instead of just nodding along when Jeremy would make a reference to a band I hadn't heard of, I started owning that I had no idea who Mumford and Sons were (don't worry, I'm now happily up to date, as my playlists show). I learned to let my goofy side show with him, and he kept loving me and reassuring me and challenging me to let him love me for me.

That lesson has been an important one as I learn how to nurture true friendships, real ones that are based on mutual appreciation and trust and intent. I admit, it's all too easy to go back to playing my internal game of hide-and-seek. After all, I carved that path for a long time, and it can feel like a familiar and safe one. But that kind of familiar, that kind of safe, only leads to lonely places. I know we've already talked about how people pleasing comes from feelings of being afraid, of craving acceptance and approval, of a misplaced desire to feel like you belong. There's one more feeling we have to add to the file when it comes to people pleasing.

And that's loneliness.

For all the feelings I've tried to avoid with my people pleasing and for all the feelings I've been seeking through my people pleasing, loneliness is one that is present at all times. It's lonely to hide in plain sight. It's lonely not to allow yourself to be fully known but also to be too afraid to let yourself be known. It's lonely to always stand behind the gate of your heart, never willing to open it up and let others in.

Lonely. Lonely. Lonely.

When you approach relationships and community with the idea that you can't ever mess up, that you can't ever be human in front of other people, you're setting yourself up for an epic case of what I call the Lonelies. It doesn't matter the size of the group of people you surround yourself with. You can be all alone in the midst of a crowd when you're worried more about messing up than you are with making progress.

And be sure and check this out. That word I kinda sorta made up, about having a bad case of the Lonelies? Look at the spelling.

Lone. Lies.

How can you know you can't let anyone see you mess up? By the lies that rattle in your head:

I can't mess up because then people will think I'm a joke.
I can't mess up because then people won't ever forget it, and they won't let me forget it either.
I can't mess up because people will think that's all I am—a mess.

Once those lies are in play, these next ones follow:

I have to do whatever it takes to not mess up.
I have to do whatever it takes to cover up any mess I do make.
It's better to sweep anything I'm struggling with under the
rug, out of sight.

And then there's the final lie of the Lonelies, the one that keeps you isolated and alone:

Once I hide my faults and my messes, I will be at no risk of
rejection, ridicule, or hurt.

That's probably the most epic lie of the Lonelies, because hiding doesn't remove those risks at all and only keeps you alone and afraid, terrified of what someone might find out.

Here's another thing I've learned, and it's not fun. Not letting you see me mess up is also about pride. I get it. It doesn't feel like pride, does it? In many ways, it feels the exact opposite. I can't let you see me mess up because I already feel plenty bad about myself, and I don't want to give you any reason to pile on. But when you stop and think about it, there is a dose of pride mixed in there.

I need you to think of me at this higher level. Not this lower level of being someone who doesn't have her stuff together.

It's strange to realize that people pleasing and pride are birds of a feather. I didn't see the connection for a long time, because I saw pride as being overly impressed with your own accomplishments and abilities, and I was nowhere near that. As a matter of fact, when I was growing up, our family had a thing about never accepting praise or appreciation from someone. If someone told me I played the piano well, I'd duck my head and respond with a comment about how my ability could only come from the Lord, or I'd point out where I could have played the piece better. Now, of course, any ability we have is because of the way God created us; it wasn't wrong for me to point to Him. But it wouldn't have been prideful to have simply thanked someone for paying me a compliment. I didn't need to talk about where I dropped a note in the fourth stanza or act like God had just dropped this ability to play the piano on me fully formed, acting like there hadn't been hours and hours of lessons and practice. I can tell you this: I was very, very proud of my humility.

———

They messed up big time but didn't want anyone to see. They thought they'd figured out a way to sweep it under the rug. Or fig leaf, in their case.

They were the first humans, the summit of God's creation. Remember how we talked about, in chapter 3, the beautiful design God has for us by building us for community and how we can see this from the very beginning, in the garden of Eden? As the first humans, Adam and Eve were also the first community. They had the perfect situation. They had each other; they had a loving Father. All their needs were provided for.

But it wasn't enough.

Adam and Eve did the one thing they were told not to do: eating the fruit of the tree of the knowledge of good and evil. Adam and Eve messed up. They messed up big. They defied God. They believed the Enemy over their Creator. You'd think they'd go running to God, apologetic and scared. Instead, they did something else.

> They heard the sound of the LORD God walking in the garden in the cool of the day, and the man and his wife hid themselves from the presence of the LORD God among the trees of the garden. (Genesis 3:8)

Did you see it? They hid. They went into hiding, embarrassed and ashamed of the exposure of their nakedness, afraid. Their response to that shame was to hide, to hide from an almighty God who surely would not be fooled.

This shows me a couple of things. Hiding is a pretty common response when we feel afraid. When we mess up, it's a standard reaction to want to hide it away. But it's hard to stay hidden.

This whole situation started with lies from the serpent in the garden who tempted them to eat from the tree. It escalated to the lie expressed by hiding. And it ultimately resulted in Adam and Eve having to leave the garden, the place of perfect expression of relationship and community with God, because they had bought into it (Genesis 3).

That's a case of the Lonelies, the Lone Lies that we've been dealing with ever since.

———

Jeremy and I were staying at the home of some friends of ours in San Antonio. Well, correction. I'd actually never met them until we stayed at their house. Jeremy had met them before, and they were so generous, so kind, that when they offered to let us stay with them for a night before we needed to catch a flight to California, we accepted.

When I tell you these people were sweet, they really were. Kind. Thoughtful. Such a great example of hospitality.

Early the next morning, Jeremy hit the shower early at about 5:00 a.m. while I packed my stuff. As I tidied up the room where we were staying, I could hear my husband's voice singing an unfamiliar song from the bathroom. It took me a minute, but then the words became clearer. He was singing, "This shower has no water pressure. This shoooooowwwwwerrrrrrr has noooooooooo water pressure. Water pressure. No water pressure." I was laughing to myself as he created a shower serenade bemoaning the lack of water pressure coming from the pipes. He wrapped up his shower, we finished getting ready, and we headed out to the living room where our hosts were waiting to see us off, ready to say our goodbyes before catching our flight.

"I'm sorry," the wife said immediately.

Excuse me?

"About the water pressure," she explained.

Jeremy and I froze in our tracks. "You could hear me?" Jeremy said.

"Well, yes," she confirmed. "Our walls are kind of thin."

If I could have sunk through the floor, I would have. We were absolutely mortified. But guess what? There was nowhere to run, nowhere to hide, no fig leaves to weave. Jeremy was busted. And you know what's great about that? We survived. He apologized. But our hosts were lovely and gracious. They thought it was hilarious. And after a quick moment of embarrassment, followed by laughter, we lived to shower another day. It was a hiccup, one that we now see as a great story. That's the thing with owning your humanness and your mistakes. It takes the air out of them. Or water pressure, depending on the situation.

That's a really important lesson for you and me. I can inflate the idea of someone seeing me mess up to become the size of a huge monster. I turn the idea of being seen for all my flaws into something that I think could devour me. But when we let our messes be seen, first in places we know are safe, and later in places where we accept the risks, it begins to shrink the reality of our failures down to size. Are you and I going to embarrass ourselves sometimes? Of course. Would it feel better to not have to own up to the weird and goofy things we do and thoughts we have? Again, yes. But the reality is, we're imperfect.

"All are from the dust," wrote the preacher in the book of Ecclesiastes, "and to dust all return" (3:20). I know I'm making progress in living with authenticity when I'm willing to take my finger and sign my name across my dusty deeds, mistakes, and missteps, not to condemn myself but rather to come out of hiding.

———

There are a whole lot of verses in the Bible that you might hear called the "one anothers." No, it's not a band name (although that could be pretty epic). It's a list of commands we're given about how we're supposed to treat each other, how we're supposed to operate as a community. It seems like we focus a lot on the one-anothers that have to do with loving each other, accepting each other, being patient with each other. And to be sure, there are lots of one-anothers on those topics.

But several of them have to do with being vulnerable and honest with each other:

"Do not lie to one another" (Colossians 3:9).
"Confess your sins to one another" (James 5:16).
"Bear one another's burdens" (Galatians 6:2).
"Having put away falsehood, let each one of you speak
    the truth with his neighbor, for we are members one of
    another" (Ephesians 4:25).

That's quite the list. And I realize that in trying to keep others from seeing your messes, you probably haven't thought of it as "lying." That seems a little harsh, right? But when you think about it, when you're leaving out the places where you struggle from the way you tell your life's story, it's false. It's not real. It's not the truth.

The game of hide-and-seek we've been playing since Adam and Eve in the garden has no winners. If I "successfully" keep you from knowing when I make mistakes, I lose authenticity in my relationship with you. When I retreat from relationship with you because I'm afraid you'll see the real me—a me I don't want to have to own up to—I lose.

I want to be clear here: I'm not suggesting that you are vulnerable with everyone. I've told you how, at times in the past, I've trusted too easily, when in an effort to be open and transparent, I've gotten burned. I've had the painful experience of thinking I was developing a friendship, where I thought I could be real with my failures and sins, only to realize the motives were off on the other person's part. They weren't there for each of us to learn to walk more closely with God, to encourage and challenge each other to come up higher. No, it was ultimately revealed that they were there because they had an agenda, a need to be associated with someone who'd been on television. They wanted to know the "dirt" for their own purposes. I get that that could sound a little severe, but it's simply the reality of a couple of these situations. Those experiences pushed me back into a hiding hole of isolation. *Hey, I stepped out there, took a chance, and it backfired*, I thought.

Well, I've got to tell you, that's part of the necessary risk of coming out of hiding. To have community, to leave behind the Lone Lies, we have to accept something up front: we are going to get burned from time to time. And here's the beauty of that: God has used those situations to teach me better discernment, and has brought relationships into my life that I value even more because they are built on genuineness.

Even Jesus experienced betrayal at the hands of one of His closest friends. Judas's betrayal of Jesus wasn't from across a distance, pointing out to the Roman soldiers who Jesus was. No, it was up close. It was personal. Judas betrayed Jesus with a kiss to the cheek (Matthew 26:48–54). Unfortunately, we're going to have times when someone we never would have expected will betray us with a kiss.

Does that mean that isolation is the answer? No. For Jesus, did that risk mean that He ditched the idea of having disciples, of having a close group of friends around Him as He lived out the purpose of His life? Nope. As a matter of fact, about the small group of people He surrounded Himself with, He said this: "No longer do I call you servants, for the servant does not know what his master is doing; but I have called you friends, for all that I have heard from my Father I have made known to you" (John 15:15). He had friends who would deny knowing Him out of their own fear. He had friends who ran away when soldiers came to arrest Him. And He also had friends who stayed with Him all the way to the foot of the cross. They were all worth the risk, as far as Jesus was concerned.

Now, you and I, we've got to be honest about our own conduct in friendships. We can't expect friends to be trustworthy if we ourselves aren't. We can't expect others to handle our vulnerability with care if we aren't careful with theirs. We need to be the kind of people we would want to be in relationship with. We need to be safe to be with. To leave hypercritical, arrogant judgment at the door. To be mature enough to handle the trail of dust others bring with them into our lives. We can't expect more out of others when it comes to our relationships than we're willing to offer.

There was a time when, if I'd been spotted and photographed almost dumping my grocery cart over in the parking lot, I would have been so embarrassed. I would have let the critical voice in my head start reciting all my clumsy, awkward history and making me relive it. But because God is so gracious to me and teaches me more and more about the delight He takes in the freedom I'm gathering, my response was different this time.

This time, as I told you, I thought it was funny when those pictures hit the internet, bags of ice sliding, me hanging on the cart for dear life. And because I was able to truly see it as funny, I laughed. A sincere belly laugh at the hilarity of the situation. A laugh that feels like a beloved battle cry of freedom.

I laughed. And then I posted it to my own social media. And I laughed and laughed some more.

Guess what? It's hard to hide when you're laughing.

I'm ready to retire from the hide-and-seek shame game I've endured for too long. There's a phrase kids call out when they're ready to end a game of hide-and-seek. It's "olly olly oxen free," one of those funny things you recognize when you hear it but have no idea what it means. There are plenty of theories on how we came to say this and what it means, but here's the one I like the best: "All ye, all ye outs in free, all the outs in free . . . ; in other words, all who are out may come in without penalty."[1] I'm ready to come out of hiding, my friend, and I hope you are too. May all of us who have been hiding our mess-ups and struggles and sins in the dark come home without penalty because our debts have been paid by Jesus Christ.

Let's Chat About It

1. Like we've talked about, we each have a particular area of people pleasing where we struggle the most. Not wanting anyone to see me mess up is an area that has kept me snagged in the past. We've got one more area to talk about in the upcoming chapter, but as of right now, what has resonated with you most?

2. What are some Lone Lies that you've believed? What would it mean to leave those falsehoods behind? What actions would you take? How would it feel to no longer be captive to those lies?

3. What is something about yourself that you've been hiding? What are you scared will happen if you bring it out into the light?

4. How can you evaluate if a possible friendship is one in which you can place your trust? Ask: What do they talk about? If they're talking about everyone else, and they're disclosing all kinds of information about other people, it's a good guess that they'll likely do the same thing to you.

5. What do you think about the connection of people pleasing and pride?

Let's finish this chapter together with these beautiful scriptures:

*At one time you were darkness, but now you are
light in the Lord. Walk as children of light.*

EPHESIANS 5:8

*The light shines in the darkness, and the
darkness has not overcome it.*

JOHN 1:5

*He has delivered us from the domain of darkness and
transferred us to the kingdom of his beloved Son.*

COLOSSIANS 1:13

Chapter 8

ARGUMENTS ARE
NOT REJECTION

WE'LL JUST HAVE TO AGREE TO DISAGREE.

Um, I'm sorry, what?

As a people pleaser, I'm allergic to conflict, disagreement, and arguments. I would do almost absolutely anything to avoid them.

Let me tell you about a personality theory that was developed in the late 1940s by a researcher named Donald W. Fiske and, over the past decades, has been explored and expanded. His idea, which was later built on by other researchers and psychologists, is that there are five basic "big" personality traits. Those personality traits are openness, conscientiousness, extraversion, agreeableness, and neuroticism.[1] When you're a people pleaser, I think it's important to pay attention to that personality trait of *agreeableness*.

On the positive side, if someone shows a lot of agreeableness in their personality, that means they are usually kind, thoughtful of others, caring, and understanding. But when that agreeableness takes on an unhealthy spin, it can turn into conflict avoidance. It can mean not standing up for what you value or believe in because staying out of a disagreement becomes more important.

When people say things like, "We'll just have to agree to disagree," it's like they're speaking Martian or something. How do you do that? To be connected, to make sure you like me, don't we have to be on not just the same page but the same paragraph and punctuation? As a friend of mine likes to say, there are two things you'll probably never see: a unicorn and a people pleaser starting an argument. For me, for far too long, an argument just felt like rejection, something I never wanted and definitely would never start.

I think I'm naturally wired to find arguments especially stressful, but I also come by it through years of my upbringing. My family life as a kid really was in some ways a lot like what you would have seen on the television screen; we just didn't argue, debate, or engage in conflict. If you thought that when the cameras turned off things turned into a cage match, well, that just wasn't the case. We lived by a mantra of, "Great! Everything's great!" My parents consistently and gently modeled a completely conflict-free environment to us.

But that also required squashing any kind of challenging conversation. Arguments were to be avoided at all costs, which meant that, more often than not, you'd have to push down any squabble or disagreement in order to maintain the peace. For some of my siblings, based on their personalities, that was probably pretty tough for them. They had questions that required complex conversations. They had opinions that would have been inconvenient to the veneer of harmony. They'd dig in from time to time, and a couple of my siblings could really get into some serious debates.

For me?

It was kinda great being in a home where non-conflict was the expectation. Not necessarily healthy, but very much my jam.

I simply don't like to argue. I don't want to risk feeling rejected. I don't want to risk upsetting anyone. Take, for example, when I'm chatting as part of a group, and two of the guys start discussing their different points of view on something. I'm immediately uncomfortable. I just can't take it. If they go on for more than a minute or two, I'll make a Jinger exit, which means, I'm out.

I don't like to have to uphold a position. I really just want people to get along, and I've long been willing to let go of what's important to me rather than fight for my voice to be heard. If I'd gone to a public high school, I never would have been on the debate team. (Is there an un-debate team in high school? 'Cuz I would have crushed that.)

There's something about disagreement that makes me feel less connected. My people pleasing has often left me on the edge of feeling like I am always at risk of you not liking me, not wanting to be around me. You add in a serving of disagreement on top of that inner dialogue, and it seemed to me that was the perfect rejection recipe. Sure, agreement was not only expected of me growing up but a big part of how I experienced approval.

As it turns out, adulting requires hard conversations. Holding firm to your faith means that you're going to make people angry sometimes. Being on social media opens you up to *a lot* of potential disagreement. Life as a human is going to have plenty of moments when you have to step up into the conflict zone, like it or not.

———

Romance was on the calendar. That was the plan.

We'd only been married a few months. Jeremy and I had saved up our pennies and had budgeted to stay over a few extra days following a speaking engagement we had out of town. We were still living in Laredo at the time but traveling out to Los Angeles for the event. It seemed like the perfect way to plan for a little second honeymoon. As part of our trip planning, we booked an Airbnb in Burbank. We'd never stayed in an Airbnb before, which only added to the anticipation of adventure.

The online pictures of the property were amazing. It was a classic California bungalow with beautiful, luscious green grass and a white picket fence surrounding the front yard. It was on a spacious corner lot. There were horses—*horses!*—on the acreage next door. Flowering vines climbed up the stucco exterior. It was super close to Warner Bros. Studios, with restaurants and shopping all around. All in, it had this amazing aesthetic with great amenities.

Sure, the price tag was a little higher than we had hoped, and my little frugal heart cringed a bit at the cost, but it was totally going to be worth it. As the event wrapped up, I couldn't wait to get to our little second honeymoon getaway. We said our goodbyes, hopped in the rental car, and followed the directions to the cute little bungalow.

When we pulled up into the drive, the first thing that hit me was the grass. Or, more specifically, the lack of beautiful, luscious green grass. The yard was dirt. All dirt. Dusty. Dry. Dirt. Where was that charming, flourishing yard?

Hm. Maybe they're getting ready to resod the yard, I thought.

The second thing I noticed was another car in the driveway. I was surprised to see another vehicle there. Jeremy stared at the other car for a second. "I think the owner planned to meet us here, to show us everything," he guessed.

Jeremy threw the rental car into park, and we walked through the dirt with our one suitcase and knocked on the door.

The door swung open, and a middle-aged woman greeted us. "Hey," she mumbled. She turned quickly, waving us in. Just inside the door was a middle-aged guy in his fifties.

Okay. Odd. Maybe he's just here so the owner isn't on her own, getting us checked into the Airbnb. Stranger danger and all that. Okay. All right.

The woman steered us around the guy and guided us to a bedroom. There was no lock on the door. "Here's your room," she drawled. We took in the view. There was the doorway we were standing in. And then there was a set of French doors across the room, a dingy sheet tacked up across the glass. Those doors didn't have locks either. The walls gave off a stale aroma. The room had the shabby part down, but not the chic. We backed out of the room, into the tiny hall.

"Here's the bathroom," the owner gestured, pointing to another door down the hallway. We peeked inside to find an ancient, crusty bathroom. "Be sure and leave the window open in the shower." We crowded into the musty bathroom so she could show us the window. "Oh, there's Rose," she gestured. She pointed out the window to a tiny little old lady wandering around some rose bushes clinging to the dirt yard, snipping off dead roses with a huge pair of scissors. "Yep, that's Rose," the owner said again. "Don't worry about her." (Cue the horror movie sound effects.)

Jeremy locked his eyes onto mine, through some kind of spousal telepathy exactly mirroring my thoughts: *What. Is. Happening?!*

The owner continued the tour, taking us back down the hallway. "Here's the kitchen. And the fridge," she explained, swinging open the fridge door.

Yes, okay, it was a fridge. We were familiar with the technology. But it was full, and I mean full, of food. She started jabbing at the contents with her finger. "You can eat some of this. But don't eat that. And you can stick some stuff here on this shelf, but leave this shelf alone."

Slowly, slowly, the gears in our brains turned over the details of the last few minutes, and then, *click*, realization dawned.

"Wait, wait, wait," Jeremy asked her. "So we're not staying here alone?"

The owner gave a sharp cackle. "No, of course not. You rented the bedroom, not the whole house," she retorted, irritation in her tone. She grumbled to herself as we followed her on the next leg of the tour, shaking her head.

"Oh, okay," Jeremy responded.

Dumb out-of-towners, we.

Both our brains were now spinning overtime. Listen, this place was pricey. Like, we-could-have-stayed-in-a-nice-hotel kind of pricey, not a shared bathroom, bedroom with no lock, Rose-in-the-backyard-with-a-potential-murder-weapon bargain.

The small living room/kitchen combo had a couch in the center of the room, facing the television. The guy in his fifties was now sitting on the couch, huge noise-canceling headphones over his ears connected to the television, munching snacks, and watching a show.

The owner noticed us noticing him. "He's not even my husband," she told us.

Oooookay.

"He's from Florida," she said, as if this would clear everything up. "He comes and stays with me for a couple of months of the year."

Things were getting weird.

"So, that's it," she wrapped up. The tour was now apparently over since the fridge boundaries had been established and the random guy on the couch had been explained. We went back to "our" bedroom, closed the door with no lock, and sat on the edge of the bed.

What are we supposed to do?! we scream-whispered to each other.

We'd made the reservation, paid our money. Undoing this whole situation was going to take a very uncomfortable conversation, one that might not end well, given the demeanor of the owner. After what seemed like the longest time, we came up with our next step. We opened the bedroom door to find Couch Guy and the owner still hanging out in the living room. "We're just gonna head out for some food," we told them. And we drove to Chipotle.

That's it. That was the whole next step at that point. When you don't know what to do with what life throws at you, sometimes all you can do is head to Chipotle.

We ordered our food, and I've got to tell you, I'd never felt more dejected. We'd built up this mini-honeymoon so big. We were several hundred dollars into this Airbnb commitment. And now we were trapped between the very real possibility of spending our romantic long weekend in a house with no locks on the doors and a parade of people hanging out and the weirdest sense of not wanting to risk a conflict with the Airbnb owner . . . or Rose . . . or Couch Guy.

We made our way back to the bungalow, and somewhere along the way, Jeremy found the resolve to undo the whole deal. We went back into the house, and Jeremy pulled the owner aside for a little conversation. "Look," he explained, "we're just not going to be able to stay here. You know, we just got married . . ."

"It's your honeymoon?!" the owner exclaimed. "That's wonderful! A honeymoon!"

We hadn't been married very long, just a few months. So it was technically second honeymoon kind of territory, but we weren't about to split hairs. We still qualified as newlyweds, and we were clinging to that in this moment.

"See," Jeremy continued, "as newlyweds, we thought we'd have the place to ourselves. We just didn't realize this was the situation, sharing a house with other people. So, we're gonna find a hotel in the area . . ."

"You should have read the description in the listing; it makes it clear you're renting a room," she argued.

"You're right, you're right," Jeremy agreed with her. "It's my bad. But we're going to have to find somewhere else to stay."

We certainly didn't want to initiate an argument with the owner. We really did feel bad about needing to ditch, and the Airbnb owner was not pleased with us. It was definitely an awkward few minutes, one of the agree-to-disagree moments I'm always trying to stay away from. We said that we were sorry for the change in plans but we stood firm. We retreated to a corner of the living room to pull out our phone and find a hotel. But the owner was now really invested in our plans. As Jeremy and I scrolled through available hotel rooms, she walked over, plucked the phone out of my hand, and said, "Ooh, where are you gonna stay? I want to see. I'll tell you the ones you shouldn't pick."

Oh, the irony.

"We'll figure it out, ma'am, thank you," Jeremy kindly told her, retrieving my phone from her grasp. We quickly grabbed that one suitcase we'd left in the bedroom and hightailed it out of there in a literal cloud of dust.

When I tell you that we felt guilty and terrible and rude and all kinds of bad, I'm not kidding. Yep. Even in the midst of a way-too-expensive unplanned stranger slumber party, even knowing we'd likely never see the owner or her fellow house squatters again, our people-pleasing ways were in full gear. But some conflicts, some tough conversations, are worth having, and this was for sure one of them.

———

I spent many years thinking that having any kind of conflict or argument was not part of a Christian lifestyle. Neither was being angry. Or risking someone getting their feelings hurt.

The combination of both my upbringing and my personality has long made me feel like being in any kind of disagreement with someone meant that I was at risk of losing their approval, their friendship, or their love.

I can see now that it's caused me to view relationships through a unique filter. To my people-pleasing mind, relationships are radically fragile. This belief in the fragility of relationships has kept me scrambling over the years to tiptoe and whisper, lest I set off a shockwave that could send a relationship crashing to the floor.

So sold was I on this idea that I really struggled to speak up on basic stuff in my marriage. Jeremy would ask my opinion on something, and my mind would race, not wanting to say anything he might disagree with. To my mind, if I said something different from what he might think, I could jeopardize the closeness of our relationship. Over the years, Jeremy has assured me again and again that he wants to know what's going on inside my head. He wants to hear my thoughts, not just a regurgitation of what I think he wants to hear.

Like we've been unpacking, our people-pleasing "techniques" have at their core our individual strategies for getting our needs met. We please because we have the dual motives to receive approval and to keep our anxieties at bay. There's nothing like an argument to completely upend the carefully constructed peace a people pleaser seeks. Arguing is the complete opposite of the people pleaser's approach to life. It's an all-out assault on our deepest sense of need, which is belonging and acceptance. Our God-given and good need for community can feel like it's getting completely hijacked in a situation where we don't feel aligned with those around us. But does being in community actually mean that we can't ever have conflict?

Should we be thoughtful and kind in our relationships? Yes. Should we intentionally push relationships to the brink by being argumentative over everything? No. But are there going to be times we're going to disagree about something and have to live in that tension?

Absolutely.

When I look at Scripture, I see Jesus having lots of uncomfortable conversations. He's not cruel. He doesn't go looking for a fight. But He's clear and straightforward in situations. He deals with things head-on. When I look at Jesus' interactions in the four books of the Gospels in the New Testament, it makes me rethink how I've looked at disagreements as something to avoid at all costs.

One time, a high-achieving young man approached Jesus and asked Him how he could attain eternal life. Jesus gave him a quick recap of high points from the Ten Commandments. The young man assured Jesus that he'd kept all these commandments from childhood. But then, watch this:

> Jesus, looking at him, loved him, and said to him, "You lack one thing: go, sell all that you have and give to the poor, and you will have treasure in heaven; and come, follow me." Disheartened by the saying, he went away sorrowful, for he had great possessions. And Jesus looked around and said to his disciples, "How difficult it will be for those who have wealth to enter the kingdom of God!" And the disciples were amazed at his words. (Mark 10:21–24)

Wouldn't it have been easier for Jesus to have just told him, "You're doing great! Keep up the good work!"? But there's a really important clue in verse 21 that I want us to look at again: "Jesus, looking at him, *loved* him, and said to him . . ."

Wait. What?

Jesus loved him. And because Jesus loved him, He couldn't let this guy go on his way without showing him the truth. The truth is that for this young man to inherit eternal life, he needed to follow Jesus. He needed to understand that no matter how well he tried to keep the commandments, it would never be enough for him to "earn" his way into heaven. Jesus knew this young man was used to achieving his way through his efforts and hard work and wealth. But that's not how the kingdom of God works. The grace of Jesus does what we cannot.

That's love right there, to tell someone the truth, even when it might burst their bubble, even when it might not be what they want to hear, or even when it may hurt your own reputation or change people's opinions about you.

It's also not lost on me that this guy didn't respond with, "Hey, thank You so much! I'm so glad You unpacked that for me! I'm going to come into agreement with everything You just said and do it!" No, the passage says that he walked off, sad and disheartened. And Jesus let him walk away, didn't debate him down, didn't try to force an agreement out of him. It shows me that I can't force someone to see things my way. My responsibility is to love them enough to tell them the truth and then let them process that. At the end of the day, it's not my job to talk them into my perspective, to present the perfect argument, or to demand that they come over to my way of thinking.

Jesus' hard conversations in Scripture often begin with someone asking a question. Sometimes, those questions are asked as a trap. Many of the religious leaders who approached Jesus were doing so with a motive, trying to bait Jesus into either saying something they could use against Him or to expose Him. Jesus responded in a variety of ways, sometimes by telling a parable to make His point, sometimes by quoting Scripture, and sometimes by calling them out for their hypocrisy.

But Jesus also wasn't wandering around looking for a good debate. He was truthful and consistent in His interactions. He knew when and how to take a verbal stand, and He also knew when not to engage with someone who was just looking for a fight.

The nineteenth-century preacher and theologian Charles Bridges said of Jesus,

Oh, for wisdom to govern the tongue, to discover the right time to speak and the right time to stay silent. How instructive is the pattern of our great Master! His silence and his answers were equally worthy of himself. The former always conveyed a dignified rebuke. The latter responded to the confusion of his contentious enemies. Will not a prayerful meditative study communicate to us a large measure of his divine wisdom?[2]

I don't think I could have any better mentor in this area than my mother-in-law, Diana. Diana is loving, kind, generous, and gracious. And she is bold in her communications about where she stands. She is clear about who she is and where her boundaries are.

Diana was raised in an incredibly dysfunctional and abusive home. She saw things no kid should be exposed to. Her strategy as a kid to stay out of harm's way was to keep her head down, to be agreeable and quiet, and to stay in her room as much as possible, practicing her violin for hours and hours a day.

When she finally moved out, it would have been understandable for her to have continued this practice of argument avoidance and conflict caution. Think about the illustration of a panic room we talked about; it would have made sense for Diana to simply emotionally rebuild a familiar panic room in her adult life as a protective measure, continuing to shield herself from hard conversations or calling out unhealthy behavior. But Diana has a vibrant, solid relationship with God; and a panic room, at the end of the day, is a dead end. She really believes what the Bible says about her worth as God's child, believing that through Jesus she can be bold and strong and free. So she is.

She understands just how damaging it would be to pass on to the next generation the survival skills she had to use in an awful home situation. That means she was willing to raise Jeremy and his siblings differently, that she was willing to build her marriage differently. For example, one time one of her kids was invited to go on an extended road trip with another family. Diana thought about it, prayed about it, and declined. The family was extremely offended that Diana turned down the offer. It caused a lot of anger, but Diana stood firm. Years later, information about this family was revealed that completely validated Diana's decision all those years before.

What if Diana had continued down a people-pleasing path, choosing not to say anything, not to listen to her maternal instinct? What if she had been more worried about a disagreement than discernment? She was willing to risk this family's anger in order to do the right thing for her child, even before history played out the way it did.

Does Diana go looking for a fight? No. But she doesn't back down from important conversations. She doesn't get trembly and shy. She's clear, fair, concise, and steady. She says what needs to be said and stands on truth. It shouldn't be surprising that now she runs a nonprofit that protects some of the most vulnerable people in our nation: children who have been affected by parental incarceration. She's turned her life journey into an opportunity to help others who are vulnerable and unable to help themselves.

I don't claim to know all the reasons the world is the way it is today. On one hand, it seems like people are picking fights all the time on online platforms, quibbling and squabbling over just about everything, waves of drama in the wakes of their social streams. On the other hand, you also see stories about a child being bullied in the street, and no one says anything; people just keep walking on by. It's like we've forgotten when to speak up, why, and how to do it. Whether people are people pleasers or not, we've forgotten the art of disagreement. We've forgotten the courage of owning a position that might not be popular while staying well clear of finger-pointing and name-calling.

———

The apostle Paul was such an interesting guy. His letters to the early churches show someone who was both boldly passionate about truth while also wanting to walk in love, kindness, and gentleness. He addressed a particular situation in the church community in a town called Philippi in the country of Greece. Paul spent time there,

Whether people are people pleasers or not, we've forgotten the art of disagreement.

teaching and helping the church, loving the people. About ten years later, Paul was in prison in Rome for his faith and, while in jail, he wrote a letter to the church at Philippi. He'd heard some concerning news about how things were going. In particular, there were two women who weren't getting along.

So Paul entered the chat.

He wrote:

I entreat Euodia and I entreat Syntyche to agree in the Lord. Yes, I ask you also, true companion, help these women, who have labored side by side with me in the gospel together with Clement and the rest of my fellow workers, whose names are in the book of life. Rejoice in the Lord always; again I will say, rejoice. Let your reasonableness be known to everyone. (Philippians 4:2–5)

In a way, Paul was willing to confront the confrontation between Euodia and Syntyche, right?

The question is, why?

As a people pleaser, I think I would have tried to stay out of whatever these women disagreed about, thinking my silence would help keep the community together. But Paul demonstrated that for the *good* of the community, something had to be said. This conflict had to be confronted. That's where you and I can get it wrong through our filter of people pleasing, this idea that ignoring problems is the best way to keep a bond. Instead, Paul went to the heart of the issue. Not only did he call out the disagreement between these two women, he also called on the community to likewise deal with the issue, with the goal of getting them to at least agree in the Lord, even if they couldn't see eye-to-eye on whatever it was they were squabbling about. Paul elevated the importance of their community of faith over the discomfort of needing to call out what could be a threat to it.

In verse 5, where Paul said, "Let your reasonableness be known to everyone," that word *reasonableness* simply means gentleness, fair-mindedness, patience. If you're like me, part of my hesitation in confronting issues is I've seen it done in a way that is harsh, belittling, arrogant, and unkind. Wanting to stay far away from that, I've gone too far to the other side, not saying anything at all. But look at the beauty of being able to talk about real issues in a real way with real compassion. There's tremendous freedom in dealing genuinely and honestly in our relationships. That's what real belonging is. That's the total opposite of rejection.

Some days it feels like God keeps giving me opportunities to grow in this area. Recently, we had to take one of our girls for some routine blood work her pediatrician wanted her to have. We were recommended to go to a place not too far from us, a medical office that did that kind of thing. So we made an appointment, loaded up the kids, and headed there. Except, it was in a rundown strip mall. It didn't seem like a medical office kind of place. The look didn't get any better once we were inside. The small lobby was dirty and cluttered. The staff were kind but disorganized. The AC was out, and the waiting room was hot and stuffy. We kept waiting for them to call our name. We waited. And we waited. And we waited.

Finally, long after our appointment's scheduled time, they called us back to a room. Then we were waiting and waiting on the doctor, all for this simple blood test. After far too many ticks of the clock, Jeremy said, "Do you really feel okay about this place? Do you want to wait anymore?"

"No," I said. "I really don't."

"Same. I'll be right back," he responded. He walked down the hall to the nurses' station to let them know that we were going to leave. I ducked my head out of the door so I could follow with the girls once he let them know we were leaving. He told the nurses that we weren't going to be able to wait any longer and that we were heading out.

Then one of the nurses, who was so nice, said, "Oh, the doctor is going to be with you in just a couple of minutes." And right as Jeremy said, "Thanks, but we're not going to stay," I said, "Okay."

Jeremy just looked at me like, *What?*

We'd made our decision, he went to act on that decision, but when someone put up an objection, particularly because they did it kindly, I started to bail.

I mean, really? I'd rather risk getting bloodwork at a sketchy strip mall doctor's office than have four seconds of awkwardness with a nurse I'll never see again? Sigh.

So how do we know what things we should take a stand on and what things we should let go of? Especially since our monitors for this kind of thing probably haven't been accurately calibrated up to this point? This is where I go back to the example of Jesus. Jesus spoke up on the things that mattered to God. He spoke up when people were being mistreated; He corrected lies with truth. He didn't pretend not to see issues in people's lives. When something wasn't right, He didn't just go with the flow. He didn't enter tough conversations out of selfishness and getting His own way, but neither did He back down on the things that mattered.

Let me share with you what I've been learning to ask myself when a confrontation seems imminent: Am I going to stay silent, or am I going to say something? If I'm staying silent, is it because I'm showing wisdom by staying out of it, or is it fear? Is this a topic that Jesus would want me to speak up about? Is this an opportunity to protect someone, to love them even if they might not like what I have to say?

Am I free to fight for what is right, even when it's hard?

I've got a long way to go. And by God's grace, I've come a long way. Every day, I'm finding my voice. Your voice is also important—taking a stand when it counts, speaking up for what is right. It's my prayer that you and I can speak over the limiting whispers of our people pleasing, finding the courage and the words to make a difference when and where it matters most.

Let's Chat About It

1. It's hard to speak up when all you want to do is avoid conflict, anger, and disagreement. For you, what is it about conflict that affects you the most?

2. What are ways that you've tried to avoid arguments in the past? Has it worked? At what cost?

3. Why do you think you might connect an argument with rejection? I know, for me, it makes me feel disconnected from the person I'm talking with, and it can also trigger my worries that I might sound dumb or they might see me as difficult or silly. What is it for you?

4. Based on what you understand about Jesus, does it surprise you to learn that He conflicted with the religious leaders of the day?

Here's a prayer for us as we learn how to use our voices for what is right:

God, I want to stand for those who need help. I want to be unafraid to face conflict when it is necessary. By Your Holy Spirit, give me the wisdom I need to overcome unhealthy people-pleasing motives when I stay silent because I don't want to risk someone's judgment or opinion. Teach me how to speak with grace and also with grit. Teach me to speak with kindness but also with righteousness. In the name of Jesus, amen.

Chapter 9

IT'S SHOWTIME!

I STARED INTO THE EYES OF THE HANDSOME GUY seated across the table from me. The lights in the restaurant were low. The hearty scent of tomato sauce and roasted garlic filled the air. Around us, other couples chatted softly, dipping fresh sourdough bread into shallow dishes of buttery olive oil. It was the perfect setting for a perfect date with a guy I was developing deeper and deeper feelings for.

Like I said, perfect.

Except for the cameraman with his lens trained on me, just over my handsome date's head. Yeah, that was a little distracting. And the big rectangular light positioned just so toward us. And the boom mic covered in a furry windscreen, swinging over the table. It's not like Jeremy's view was any better. He was likewise staring across the table at me, another cameraman over my shoulder.

Our fellow diners? They were extras, enticed to come fill the restaurant that had been rented out for the evening with the promise of a free dinner and the chance to appear in the background of the show.

The camera and sound guys made final adjustments. The producer called, "Action!" And so, date-night-on-demand began.

Jeremy and I would chat for a few minutes, and the director would call, "Cut!" A few more adjustments would be made, the camera guys picking up other shots they needed. Jeremy and I were instructed to repeat some of the same conversation and gestures we'd made in the previous set. Shoot, stop, reset, the loop of a television show production shoot creating the rhythm of our interactions.

Early days, first meals together, making small talk—the process of getting to know someone can feel a little awkward. But I would say that there's probably not an adequate word for describing the unique kind of awkward it is to go through that whole process with cameras shoved in your faces and someone interrupting you when the conversation is just starting to flow.

Fast-forward a few months, and I found myself walking down the staircase in my house toward Jeremy, anticipating that we might be about to make our relationship official. I took each stair carefully, smiling at Jer, butterflies in my stomach, excited to hear what he would say to me when I got to the bottom of the stairs.

"Cut! Jinger, go back up the stairs, please! We need to start over to get the shot."

Okay.

Back up the stairs I went, waiting for my cue. I came down the stairs again, finally reaching Jeremy. He asked me to be his girlfriend, the sweetest moment. And then we got to do it all over again because there was a mic issue. And then we had to do some more takes. And then we had to do cutaways.

For me, navigating those performance expectations with the camera crew, right in the middle of my real life, whether I was about to become someone's girlfriend or I was brushing my teeth on a random Tuesday morning, was totally normal. It was all I had known since the age of ten. For Jeremy, for some of my brothers-in-law who had joined the family by this point, it was anything but.

By now you know me well enough to know that my brand of people pleasing has veered toward isolating myself, hiding away and keeping myself insulated from possible conflict and criticism. Maybe that resonates with you. But depending on your temperament, your people pleasing might look more like feeling you have to always be "on," that you always need to be putting on a show for everyone. You might feel like you need to go bigger than anyone else when it comes to giving gifts and doing favors and volunteering. Maybe for you it looks like staying later than everyone else at work. Maybe it's always putting on a happy face, no matter what is happening. The focus is on making the outside of your life as approval-ready as possible for anyone you might encounter.

But on the inside? You feel gross. You might be filled with anxiety, anger, stress. You know there are a lot of things you're putting out there, trying to prove you've got it all together. But you know you feel like you're close to falling apart. It's like living life on a movie set; the exteriors of your house look charming and cozy and compliment-worthy. But it's a facade, a face slapped up over what feels like a whole lot of empty.

———

Jesus entered the city of Jerusalem a few days before He would be arrested and crucified. Now, if you had been there to see Him arrive in the city, you would have never guessed that things would turn so quickly against Him in the next few days. When He came into Jerusalem, people were thrilled. Something like a parade route quickly developed, with Jesus riding on a donkey through the city streets and the people waving palm fronds to welcome Him (Matthew 21).

He spent the next few days in the city teaching important lessons and confronting the hypocrisy He found among a lot of the religious people. There were two groups in particular whom Jesus really called out. They were the scribes and the Pharisees (Matthew 23).

The scribes were what we would probably think of as lawyers today. They knew all the ins and outs of the religious law. They handled the legal side of things when it came to drawing up marriage certificates, property deeds, loan papers, and things like that. And they also were the ones who copied out Old Testament scriptures, and they helped interpret what Scripture said.[1]

The Pharisees were a religious group who loved following rules, just not always the ones Scripture laid out for them. They had come up with their own ideas about how to be righteous, and they held people to an extra standard. They made all kinds of decisions about who was in and who was out, based on how well someone was following their rules.[2]

Jesus had a lot of things to say about both these groups in the days He spent in Jerusalem prior to His arrest, including something that sounds a whole lot like the issue of making your external life one big show. Jesus said, "Woe to you, scribes and Pharisees, hypocrites! For you are like whitewashed tombs, which outwardly appear beautiful, but within are full of dead people's bones and all uncleanness. So you also outwardly appear righteous to others, but within you are full of hypocrisy and lawlessness" (Matthew 23:27–28). The custom at the time was to paint the tombs around the city with a limewash right at the time of year when Jesus came to Jerusalem. That whitewashing made the outside of the tombs look bright and fresh, but the reality was that there was death and decay on the inside.

Why would Jesus say such a tough thing to the scribes and Pharisees? Because He knew their inner lives didn't line up with their outward appearances. They *looked* holy. They looked like pillars of the community. They looked like they were doing all kinds of good things.

But it was all a show.

As you can imagine, the scribes and Pharisees weren't too thrilled with Jesus calling them out. In fact, a group of them began calling for Jesus' arrest, just a handful of days after He had been praised while entering the city.

We'll do just about anything, won't we, to keep up the show? When we people please from a motive of keeping up appearances, our theme song is, "The show must go on!"

At the core of this component of people pleasing is the grab for perfection. People throughout the centuries have long had a drive for theater and show when it comes to how they present their lives. But I have to say, like never before, we are continuously bombarded with images and content that puts perfect images and lifestyles before our eyes. All that exposure to perfectly curated everything has changed our eyesight and our expectations. We're overexposed to overexposed media. It's no wonder we lose sight of what's real and what's not.

We're allowing our sense of who we are to be replaced by a statement of what we should be, one generated by algorithms and marketers, impossible standards for our waistlines and closets and budgets and emotions to keep up with. We take all that messaging down into the marrow of our bones and let the dissatisfaction that's generated there become the fuel for our onstage characters.

I can tell you this: all the effort required to keep playing these parts of perfect businesswoman, perfect mom, perfect spouse, perfect friend, perfect interior designer, perfect cook, perfect workout girl, perfect daughter, perfect perfect perfect? It's wearing us out. It's worn me out.

Statistically, women my age report that they are more burned out than other age groups, more worn out than men of the same age.[3] The question is, why? After all, as women, we have more women ahead of us in age who've navigated our modern waters, the pressure on women in work and motherhood and marriage. So many of those women have really helpful insight and wisdom. It's not like we're encountering challenges and issues they haven't. So why are we feeling even more depleted?

A friend of mine was reflecting on her early motherhood experiences. When she first became a mom, the internet and social media weren't really a thing. She still felt the push for a level of perfection, but as she tells it, she was only getting a parenting magazine and a home decor magazine once a month in the mail. She wasn't confronted daily with all the ways she was coming up short.

Fast-forward to today, and we can't get away from a constant stream of comparison and conversation about how things "should" be. And the standards keep getting higher. Lately, there's been a whole lot of pushback on one social media platform where "restocking" videos for refrigerators and pantries are all the rage, with aesthetic food and cleaning and household products being organized into display-like department-store perfection, right in the family home. You can't even go into your own cabinet for a bowl of cereal these days without feeling like you're coming up short. But what about the realities of grocery budgets, a kitchen without a pantry, and a fridge you're just thankful is still working? The standards keep getting higher while the living standards of our hearts are strained far past the point of true peace.

So we spend and we film and we post and we posture, joining in the expanding chorus of perfect house, perfect wife, perfect life.

———

Of all the aspects of people pleasing we've talked about so far, this one might not feel as serious as the others. Trading down from the relationships we could have, dealing with our inside critic, the weight of avoiding necessary confrontation, the pain of hiding away from others—the costs are obvious and high. But this performance component of people pleasing? It can be a little trickier to count the cost because this is the one that can make us look so good.

After all, who doesn't love a good filter?

I've got to admit, it's fun to take an image of myself and clean it up a little. Here's a lash and brows filter; ooohhh, lookie there! Nice! What about a warm filter, make the colors pop a bit? Done!

We're so accustomed now to filtering our image, our lives, our houses, our jobs. We live in an ironic age that talks all the time about authenticity and vulnerability while at the same time manipulating our online lives, our pictures, our "personal branding." We're performing all the time, and we hardly even realize it.

But there is a significant cost to all that image scrubbing. We lose sight of reality. We forget what we really look like, how we really feel, who we really are. We can become so much more enamored with this cartoon of ourselves we've created than the unique, beloved individual God created us to be.

There's an example in the Bible, at the time the church was just beginning to grow after Jesus went back to heaven. The church was experiencing an incredible time of connection. The message about Jesus and His love was spreading. And the community of Christians was loving and serving one another at such an incredible level. There were people selling their homes and other assets and bringing those funds to the leaders of the church so everyone in the church would have the things they needed. They were taking care of each other, and the church was blossoming.

One couple in that community also had some property. Their names were Ananias and Sapphira and, at first blush, they did something for the church that seemed incredibly generous. They sold that property, and then Ananias brought the money to the church leaders. So far, so good. That was a wonderful thing to do. But then, tragedy struck.

Peter, one of Jesus' disciples and friends, was a leader in the church, and he was the one Ananias brought the money to. But Peter knew Ananias had held back some of the money from the sale of the property. That in and of itself wasn't a problem. The problem was that Ananias was making a show of acting like he had brought the full sale amount. Peter said to him, "Ananias, why has Satan filled your heart to lie to the Holy Spirit and to keep back for yourself part of the proceeds of the land? While it remained unsold, did it not remain your own? And after it was sold, was it not at your disposal? Why is it that you have contrived this deed in your heart? You have not lied to man but to God" (Acts 5:3–4).

And then Ananias, caught with his filter down, died.

Now, Sapphira, Ananias's wife, wasn't with him when he went to give that portion of money to the church leaders. But before Ananias had left to put on his big generosity show, he had told Sapphira that he wasn't going to give all of it, just part of it. They would look like super-spiritual heroes in the church's eyes, but they'd have some extra in their pockets, no one the wiser. She signed off on the plan.

About three hours after Ananias had presented the filtered money to the church leaders, Sapphira showed up. She didn't know about Ananias's fate. Peter said, "Tell me whether you sold the land for so much." And she said, "Yes, for so much." But Peter said to her, "How is it that you have agreed together to test the Spirit of the Lord? Behold, the feet of those who have buried your husband are at the door, and they will carry you out" (Acts 5:8–9). And, you guessed it, Sapphira also fell dead.

Look, I know that's a shocking story about Ananias and Sapphira. And God did not always deal with people trying to deceive the church that way. But there does seem to be a particular severity for those who were putting on a show, those who were lying about themselves to impress others. It's who Jesus was the harshest with during the time of His ministry here on earth. There's just something about being one thing but acting like you're another that keeps us far from the heart of God.

I see this echoed in our culture. Think about the number of times in the news you hear about someone in ministry or politics who has been living a double life. Once the real story comes out, the response of the public is huge and angry and loud. When someone puts up a front that we believe and admire and aspire to, the blow feels far harder when we find out it wasn't real, or, at least, that a lot of it wasn't real. Sure, all the world's a stage, but so is the backstage. What we do in all those places matters.

Jesus said, "Beware of the scribes, who like to walk around in long robes, and love greetings in the marketplaces and the best seats in the synagogues and the places of honor at feasts, who devour widows' houses and for a pretense make long prayers. They will receive the greater condemnation" (Luke 20:46–47). In this level of pretending, people use spiritual environments and communities for their own benefit. This seems especially atrocious to Jesus, because it takes advantage of other people, all for the sake of keeping up appearances.

You might think, *Well, Jinger, sure, I'm putting up something of a front. I won't be caught dead without my contouring makeup on. And sure, my husband and I argued the entire drive to our Bible study small group the other night and then acted all lovey-dovey when we walked in the door. But I'm not taking advantage of anyone. I'm not hurting anyone.*

But you are. You're hurting yourself.

There's a style of acting called method acting, when an actor tries to fully embody the character they are portraying. They're not just crying during a scene; they're taking on the full emotions and trauma of the character's backstory. For example, when the actor Al Pacino played the character of a man who was blind, he had the film crew treat him, on camera and off, as if he were blind. He stayed in character even when he wasn't on the set, continuing to act as if he was someone without sight.[4]

While this approach to acting has turned out some incredible performances, it's also very controversial. Researchers say that those who immerse themselves in their characters are more likely to lose track of their true selves. They may begin acting out in ways that are based on the character they played, long after the cameras have stopped rolling. There is concern that individuals who approach their work this way could be putting their mental health in danger. And the deepest concern is that the actor loses their sense of who they really are.[5]

It seems to me that method acting is sort of like what you and I do when we try to create a flawless performance. We immerse ourselves in what we think are the expectations of our churches, our workplaces, our romances, and our friendships. We research all the ways we think perfection looks and sounds. We seek to convince others that we truly embody this character we have created.

We are using others as our audience, and their approval is our applause, our validation that we're getting the character right.

Sometimes we've created this character by our own people-pleasing ways. And sometimes we've been raised in environments where all this acting was just part of the deal. I get that my situation is a little unique; being raised with a camera in your face tends to make you think a lot about how you're coming across. I naturally have a pretty expressive face and have some strong facial reactions to something I find funny or something I don't like. From an early age, I had to start thinking about how those expressions were coming across on the television screen because we'd sometimes have to redo something if my expressions got away from me. For you, it could have been that you were raised in a family where appearances were everything. You had to dress a certain way, present yourself a certain way. And now that you're out of your childhood home, you're not even sure what it means to not be performing all the time.

It takes me back to what we were talking about earlier, that place of feeling burnout. For me, that's one of the most consistent signals that I'm spending too much time trying to create some perfect image. The energy it takes to keep all that up. The crash that's inevitably going to come. That would be my question to you. How tired are you?

I think that's why I cherish these words of Jesus so much: "Come to me, all who labor and are heavy laden, and I will give you rest" (Matthew 11:28). Remember the scribes and Pharisees we talked about earlier, the ones who were putting on a show and creating all kinds of rules and standards beyond what God had said? Jesus was speaking these words of rest to the people who had been under the thumb of those expectations. He invited them to come out from under all those man-made requirements of performance.

He went on to say, "Take my yoke upon you, and learn from me, for I am gentle and lowly in heart, and you will find rest for your souls. For my yoke is easy, and my burden is light" (vv. 29–30). When we walk with Jesus, we don't have to act, pretend, and perform. And when we aren't spending our time and energy on acting like someone else, we have the focus and attention to do far greater things.

We've spent some time in some of the other components of people pleasing, looking at the selfish motives for those behaviors. With this performance kind of people pleasing, the self-absorbed side of it seems pretty obvious, right? When you're constantly thinking about how you're coming across and when you're constantly having to stay in character, you're really living in your own head, in a world you've confined to a limited stage.

But there's another kind of selfish that shows up—one you might not have noticed. When I participate in perfection playacting, I'm creating a standard. I'm keeping the acting going, and that facade gets added to the further fabrication of a community. Before you know it, I'm adding to the lie others are trying to achieve. None of us can really carry perfection, but we all keep trying to heft it up on our shoulders. And anytime I'm putting forward an inauthentic face, I'm adding a brick to the bag.

We've been mainly looking at the issue from a perspective of trying to make ourselves look good, look better than we really are. The other side of that tendency is putting on a skin of the long-suffering, wronged, ever-hurt sufferer. We can use this role to zap away any responsibility we have in a situation. Let's say, for example, we snap at the cashier at our local store. We're not the bad guy; they are. They were rude. They were inattentive. We'd already been in that line for too long. The store is disorganized; the staff is rude. On and on we go, playing the role of someone who was so, so wronged, regardless of what we may have done in the situation.

We act like we have the perfect marriage to push away the reality that we're not so great with mature reactions and forgiveness.

We act like we have the perfect kids to push away behavior issues and challenges.

We act like we're the perfect friend, even when we have a trail of abandoned friendships that have ended badly and abruptly. We act like we're loving our "dream job," even when things are going sideways with our boss, and the work is gutting us.

We can use all that method acting to push away our part and our responsibility and our need for growth and help.

Here's another caution for us to take to heart. There's a big difference between being self-conscious, which can lead to our performing, and being self-aware. Sometimes, when people are trying to overcome a performance mentality, they can go to a place where they just don't care anymore. They'll say anything that comes to mind, no matter who is in the room who could be hurt or offended. They'll come super late to a coffee because "that's just who I am." They'll snatch the last cookie, say the hurtful thing, tease with a bite, and track mud onto freshly mopped floors because they are being their #authenticself.

Now, come on. Laying aside our "It's showtime!" kind of people-pleasing ways in no way means that we're now cleared to be rude, thoughtless, and careless. I even see this showing up in our faith communities. People understandably get tired of the performance aspects of some religious systems. I get it, because I sure did in the harmful, overbearing, legalistic theology I was raised in. But the cure for that isn't to become all impulse and no kindness, all whim and no wisdom. Moving away from inauthentic, performance-based holograms of ourselves doesn't mean we also move away from the responsibilities we have for growing in our own maturity and in the relationships we have with our fellow humans.

"I therefore, a prisoner for the Lord, urge you to walk in a manner worthy of the calling to which you have been called," wrote the apostle Paul, "with all humility and gentleness, with patience, bearing with one another in love, eager to maintain the unity of the Spirit in the bond of peace" (Ephesians 4:1–3). If you're a believer in Jesus like I am, we actually do have a real responsibility to represent Him everywhere we go. That doesn't mean we have a responsibility to make everyone happy. It doesn't mean we have to take on a certain persona that is inauthentic to who we are. What it does mean is that we treat others with respect, that we are humble and gentle. And real. Because we are the image-bearers of Christ.

In a very real sense today, you and I are always somewhat on stage. There are cameras everywhere. There are people watching—not as much as we think they are, but still. I'll probably always be keeping an eye out. I was caught off guard just the other day. My in-laws were in town for a visit and my mother-in-law encouraged me to go out for a little me time. "You go on," she said. "I'll keep the kids." So what's a mom of two young kids to do with some me time? I bet you already know the answer.

That's right. I headed to TJ Maxx.

Now, when I tell you I looked rough, I mean it. I had been working on projects around the house that day and hadn't planned on going anywhere. I had some four-day-old hair going on that day for which a messy bun would have been an upgrade. I was dressed in workout clothes. While we do often encounter photographers on our family outings, it's not too often that I get recognized here in LA by the general public. Even when I do, because it's LA, I don't get approached that often. But on this day, as soon as I walked in the doors of the store for some retail therapy, a mom and daughter approached me. They were so sweet, saying, "Hi, Jinger! We really love you and your show!" They were really kind, and we chatted for a few minutes before going our separate ways. And I'll tell you, I was a little worried that with my crazy hair and sweaty clothes I could have made a bad impression.

But I was reminded again that it was my authentic interaction with this mom and daughter that was the real stuff. It was my attitude toward them, the way I treated them, that was far more important than if I looked put together for my TJ Maxx run or not. I don't have to be cheery smiley happy. I don't have to be all spiritual seriousness. I don't have to be projecting a fake upbeatness, and I don't have to be sophisticated. I can just be Jinger, the mom hitting up the Maxx, the girl who wrestles grocery carts, messes up band names, has days she's happy, and has days she's overwhelmed. I'm just me. And when I'm just me, a thankful and redeemed child of God, letting the light of Christ shine through, I don't have to put on a performance.

Let's Chat About It

Some of us are more prone to hide in an effort to avoid criticism, like we talked about earlier, while some of us tend to perform most of the time, always on stage, trying to earn what our hearts are longing for.

1. Where are some areas you feel like you're performing, that the reality of your life, your marriage, your career, your parenting really isn't what it seems from the outside?
2. What are you hoping to receive from others in return for that performance? Is it working?
3. What would it look like for you to be real about your life?
4. What efforts could you set aside if you weren't trying to keep up a certain appearance?

Here are some scriptures for us to tuck in our hearts, ready to be remembered the next time we're tempted to put on a performance instead of residing in reality:

> *The LORD sees not as man sees: man looks on the outward appearance, but the LORD looks on the heart.*
> 1 SAMUEL 16:7

> *Create in me a clean heart, O God, and renew a right spirit within me.*
> PSALM 51:10

> *Would not God discover this? For he knows the secrets of the heart.*
> PSALM 44:21

Chapter 10

THE SOLUTION MIGHT SURPRISE YOU

YOU CAN ACTUALLY SEE IT FROM SPACE, RIGHT THERE on the satellite images.

Just over the mountain from where Jeremy and I live, a few miles up the Antelope Valley Freeway into the high desert, is a phenomenon unlike any other. Each spring, poppies bloom under the spring sunshine, and it turns the foothills of the valley into a sea of orange-red petals. It's called the superbloom, and it's incredible. We knew we wanted the girls to experience the magic of it, so we loaded the kids and plenty of snacks up in the car and headed to the high desert, to the Antelope Valley California Poppy Reserve.

The views did not disappoint. Acres and acres of land that usually wear a lumpy beige of tumbleweeds and sand were transformed into a lush carpet of saffron. We pulled over, and the girls couldn't wait to get out of the car to run along the paths through the poppy blossoms. We took pictures, marveled at God's paintbrush, and hiked longer than I thought we could have with two little kids. It was like being on some kind of fantastical, otherworldly movie set, the scenery so vibrant it almost didn't seem real.

It was when we were coming back down a path toward the car that I realized things weren't all just sunshine and flowers. Jeremy was walking ahead of me and had put one of the girls up on his shoulders to carry her, and she was chattering in his ear. That's when I saw it from the corner of my eye, just ahead: a huge rattlesnake.

Rattlesnakes love to hide out under the blossoms of the poppies. The sun is warm after the winter, and they blend into the desert sand beneath the plants. We'd been careful while we were walking with the girls that day, but right there, right along the path, tucked just under the flowers and scrub brush, was a deadly reptile. When I tell you it freaked me out, it freaked me out.

Jeremy was calm throughout the whole thing. He explained to the girls where the snake was, pointing it out. He showed them that the snake was moving away from the path and that it wasn't coiled or acting like it was threatened. He handled the whole thing like a champ, even managing to get a video.

But . . . blegh. It still gives me the freezing shivers every time I think about it.

While the Antelope Valley is known for its poppy superbloom, it's also known year-round for rattlesnake bite treatment and study at its hospital.[1] Here's one of the craziest things to me: one of the top ways to treat a snakebite is with antivenom, which, wait for it, is made from snake venom. The very thing you're trying to heal someone from, when used in the right doses in the right situations, is the very medicine they need.

You and I have been on a journey exploring all the ways people pleasing has marked our lives, the variety of ways in which we clam up, sit out, overperform, isolate, and trade down from the best of how God wants us to live. We've had to take a hard, honest look at ourselves, at the selfish motives that have lurked just beneath the blossoms of all of our good deeds and desperate efforts. While your style of people pleasing likely looks a little different from mine, we've both identified that it's a problem in our lives, one that keeps us from living fully. It's gotten a little uncomfortable at times, right? This process of having to candidly look at how we've been living and behaving and why. But you've pressed through, and I honor your honesty and courage.

So what now? Now that we've brought all these things up to the surface, what are we supposed to do? What are the next steps?

I think the solution might surprise you.

The solution to being a people pleaser is . . . to be a people pleaser.

I know, I know, that can sound like the last thing you want to do, given what all we've been digging up. It kind of feels like realizing you have a snakebite in the form of people pleasing, going to get treatment for it, and being told that you're going to be given more snake venom. But stay with me. Remember when we talked about how we are designed for community, that we are designed to need one another? Can I just tell you? That kind of approach is the theme song of a people pleaser who is still broken, who hasn't found freedom from unhealthy people pleasing but is only walling herself in even further.

To be free from the desperate, agenda-filled, approval-seeking claws of unhealthy people pleasing means that you are free to now care for and help your fellow human beings from a place that demands nothing of them; you serve for the joy of serving.

Here's why taking the antivenom to people pleasing is so important. It seems to me that in our churches and communities, we're doing a better job talking about the burnout a lot of us feel. We're opening up the dialogue around how we've created these weird expectations for people to live up to, expectations that Jesus certainly didn't put on us. We've tried to create insulation around ourselves from those who are negative toward us. In all of it, we've been trying to make ourselves feel better. We say things like,

Just get your validation from God, and everything will be okay.

Jesus is your true identity; focus on that.

Why care about what other people think when Jesus loves you the way you are?

Those haters don't matter anyway; just forget about it and forget about them.

Those statements? They're true, and they can go a long way in helping us reframe our thoughts. But when those statements are embraced without including how God designed us, how He intentionally created us to need each other, we put ourselves at risk of falling into the same habits as before.

So what does healthy people pleasing look like?

It will be sacrificial at times.

It won't always be convenient.

It won't always be reciprocal.

It will fill you with a sense of peace and joy because it will be the Holy Spirit working through you.

You will move into relationships from a position of strength, not of desperation.

It allows you to honor well the primary relationships God has given you responsibility for, in your marriage, with your kids, your family, and your work, while still serving others.

There are some things on that list that seem awesome, right? I could absolutely get on board with some extra peace and joy. Strengthened relationships. That all sounds great.

And . . . there are some things on the list that you might not be quite as excited about but that are still an important part of loving and serving others well.

Let's unpack all of that.

Because you and I have been operating in an unhealthy form of people pleasing, we're going to need a change in how we see things. Learning to see things through new eyes is exciting and sometimes a little unsettling. Some things might look a little familiar, and other things are completely brand-new. For me, it was a learning curve to be able to identify healthy people pleasing versus the version I'd long been trapped by. I'd been so blind to my motives for so long that it took me a while to be able to distinguish the difference.

I have a kind of three-step filter in how I look at this now. First, when I'm in my unhealthy people pleasing, at its core, I'm doing and saying and worrying and analyzing all my interactions with other people through that hunger, that desperation of trying to get what I need out of the situation. But it's not a quick jump to the healthy kind of people pleasing that is our good medicine, that is the cure. There's an interim part, what I think of as a second step, that I see a lot of people go through, that I can get stuck in if I'm not careful.

Our step two is to ask ourselves, "Does this serve me?" I've seen plenty of advice on how to evaluate how and when we're going to serve through this filter. I've even seen this come up within churches. At first blush, it seems sort of reasonable, kind of protective. But there's a problem, and it's a big one.

That conscious question of "Does this serve me?" is actually the same one we didn't even realize we were asking back in the heaviest of our people-pleasing ways. It was there. It may have sounded a little different. It may have come more in the form of, "What if they don't like me? What if they cut me out? What if I sound dumb?" But if you boil all that down to its essence, you're left with the sludge of trying to get your needs met, your needs served, instead of doing for others from a clear heart. So if all you and I do is transition from unconsciously to consciously asking that question, we haven't moved that far up the path from the swamp we've been stuck in.

Once we understand evaluating why we're interacting with other people, whether that's still back in the first step (decide not to act from our desperateness) or from a conscious place of thinking first of ourselves, we can move on to the better approach. The third step is the one that understands the beauty of serving others without first running it through a filter of what we expect to receive from them.

The apostle Paul gave us a great way of checking our motives at the door. He wrote about checking our intent in Ephesians 6:6–8, reminding us we are to serve "not by the way of eye-service, as people-pleasers, but as bondservants of Christ, doing the will of God from the heart, rendering service with a good will as to the Lord and not to man, knowing that whatever good anyone does, this he will receive back from the Lord, whether he is a bondservant or is free."

Okay, this is a pretty intense passage of scripture, and I want to take a minute to break it down because it is so full of amazing stuff. What did Paul mean with that phrase at the beginning of this passage, "not by the way of eye-service"? It simply means that you're doing something to be seen by others.[2] It might not be something you would do on your own, but when people who are in authority over you (or people you've given authority in your life because you want their approval so badly) are watching, you play the part.

And then, do you notice the phrase "people-pleaser" in the passage? Yep, there it is, right in the middle of the Bible. In the language in which Paul wrote this letter, in the Greek, it means "studying to please man, courting the favor of men."[3] This is exactly the kind of people pleasing we want to stay away from. It doesn't mean that people won't end up appreciating or admiring what we do; sometimes that does happen. It means we're not purposefully seeking that, that we're not performing eye-service, that we're not studying others for the purpose of gaining their favor.

Instead, we see this place of serving others as something we do out of our love for God.

You've got to love the powerful ways Paul conveyed these ideas in his writing. It clears away so much of the agenda we often bring.

Let's face it: what often looks like serving other people can come with a whole lot of attention. There are tax breaks for contributing to nonprofits doing important humanitarian work. News features are published on someone who comes to the aid of a person who is destitute or is hurting. Service awards are given to those who go above and beyond. I'm not saying we can completely escape the attention that might come from some of the things we do for others. I'm not saying we should only serve in ways that keep us anonymous. I'm not saying people shouldn't acknowledge and thank those who do serve. What I am saying is that if that kind of attention is the main driver, it's an issue.

When we help take care of others, when we go out of our way, share what we have, show up, listen, and love well, when we do it from simply wanting to show our love and gratitude to our good God, it clears the toxic fumes of unhealthy people pleasing and becomes a perfume of pleasing people, showing them they matter, showing them the love of Christ.

I'm all about a good before and after. And when we clean out the mess we've made of our selfish people pleasing and show up for the right reasons, it's an upgrade like no other.

"Well, Jinger," you might ask, "what about boundaries?"

Fair question. As I shared with you, sometimes healthy people pleasing is inconvenient, not on the schedule, not always well received, and you won't always get a thank-you. I've seen people, and you probably have too, who seem to be serving for all the right reasons but who run themselves into the ground, with kids and spouses who grow resentful and weary of all that "doing good." (Remember the serial servers we talked about back in chapter 4?) So how do we serve, understanding that it will require sacrifice, without dishonoring the family and the community God has placed us in?

One of the first things we need to talk about is how we define boundaries. That word is getting thrown around a lot today. I'll see a meme make the rounds, saying something like, "You have to talk to me *this way.* That's my *boundary*!" or "No one gets to treat me like *this.* I have *boundaries*!" I've seen people use the word *boundaries* as a way of marking their preferences and expectations of behavior from others. That can easily become an excuse to be selfish in how we view others. We need to remember that Jesus didn't come to be served, but to serve (Matthew 20:28). But appropriate boundaries—if we must use that term—are really about determining when certain situations may actually become unsafe. Some people may cross a line and require you to set up boundaries of protection in a relationship. But having healthy boundaries doesn't mean you won't ever be inconvenienced. It doesn't mean your schedule is always the priority. It doesn't mean you get to dictate others' behavior. God is a God who knows that we sometimes grow more from the interruptions and irritations and inconveniences in our lives than from the predictable.

People are going to make demands of you. There are always going to be more opportunities to serve than we can feasibly get to. Jesus talked about the challenge of this during His time of ministry here on earth. As the time was getting closer to His arrest and crucifixion, a follower made an extravagant and expensive gesture. She brought a valuable jar of perfume to a home where Jesus was eating a meal with some of His friends. She broke open the jar and poured the perfume over Jesus' head. Because the perfume was so costly, some at the dinner complained about her actions, saying that the money spent on that perfume could have been used for taking care of the poor. But Jesus explained to them, "Leave her alone. Why do you trouble her? She has done a beautiful thing to me. For you always have the poor with you, and whenever you want, you can do good for them. But you will not always have me. She has done what she could; she has anointed my body beforehand for burial" (Mark 14:6–8).

Was Jesus being casual about the plight of the poor? Not at all.

He encourages His followers to help take care of the poor; the need is so great that it's always present. But He was also reminding His friends that He wouldn't always be with them, and this beautiful, extraordinary service that this woman had generously given was an important moment as Jesus prepared to go to the cross.

This reminds me that I need to be watching and listening for where God wants me to serve. The time we have each been given on this earth is valuable, and deciding where we pour out that time, where we extravagantly give it, is an important responsibility. While looking for the needs around me, I also need to remember that my children will only be this age once, that the level of care they need from me right now is important. I need to keep my marriage a priority, protecting and investing in it so Jeremy and I can then serve from a place of health and love. Yes, these are the people who mean the most to me in the world, my husband and my kids, and serving them is an important way that I serve God.

Paul wrote, "If anyone does not provide for his relatives, and especially for members of his household, he has denied the faith and is worse than an unbeliever" (1 Timothy 5:8). John, the disciple that we talked about who was Jesus' closest friend, had this to say: "If anyone has the world's goods and sees his brother in need, yet closes his heart against him, how does God's love abide in him? Little children, let us not love in word or talk but in deed and in truth" (1 John 3:17–18). Paul hit this topic again in his letter to the believers living in Galatia when he wrote, "As we have opportunity, let us do good to everyone, and especially to those who are of the household of faith" (Galatians 6:10).

I bring this up because I think we can get so focused on the valid huge humanitarian need out there that we forget to serve those within our own communities, or we discount the impact God can make through our finite time and efforts. I think missions and inner-city work and food banks are so, so important. I have served in these ways, and I hope to serve more. But sometimes, we can be drawn to things that are dramatic and big and feel urgent. Sometimes opportunities come into the spotlight, and people clamor to get on board, drawn by the momentum and energy of the cause.

Is it wrong to serve in those settings? No. But other places and spaces, quieter and beneath the radar, also matter. The young woman in your church who has just discovered that she's going to have to be a single mom and sole breadwinner for her kids. The elderly man who has just lost his wife of fifty-three years and is now lonely, needing someone to sit across a coffee-shop table with him for an hour each week. The teenager who is struggling in their faith walk and asks to talk to you about their struggles. Are we willing to be inconvenienced and interrupted for those moments? Do we believe God provides the direction, resources, energy, and insight for all these situations, whether we see them, in our humanness, as significant or small?

Serving from the right place, from the right heart, requires wisdom, openness, and a willingness before God to let Him show us where we can truly please people with our love, understanding, and compassion.

Jeremy reminded me of a verse that captures so beautifully the journey of moving from unhealthy people pleasing to a people pleasing that brings life and joy. It's found in the book of Proverbs: "All day long [the sluggard] craves and craves, but the righteous gives and does not hold back" (Proverbs 21:26). When you and I were people pleasing from that place of starving for attention and approval, we could never find the satisfaction we craved, even with all our efforts. We operated out of scarcity and fear. When we give to others now, in ways that seem little, in ways that feel big, now that we know better, now that we can see, we can give with a fullness of generosity and joy. Because we know we give not from our own efforts and agendas but because God empowers and guides us.

When our girls were babies, they did this hilarious thing as they became more and more aware of people's responses to them. They would cough, a cute little baby cough. It started when someone in the room would legitimately cough or clear their throat. You could see their little baby brains processing that sound. Over time, they each started learning to make that sound whenever they wanted, not just in response to a genuine tickle in their throats, but to get our attention. It was an on-demand kind of coughing, and they each were pretty delighted with their little acting skills.

As you and I move from our experience as people pleasers who were snakebit by the wrong motives into the healing and fullness of being people pleasers who serve and love from a heart made whole, we can't expect to jump from being babies to full-fledged grown-ups. Because the cure for people pleasing is people pleasing, we've got to stay vigilant in searching our motives and our hearts. Some of the activities of the two types of people pleasing can look the same. It's like our girls giving a little cough, just like they saw the big people do. It looked and sounded the same, but it was for the purpose of getting us to notice them.

I want to leave you with a few thoughts on observing yourself, observing what you're doing and why as you try on this idea of a different kind of people pleasing. Now that you are adjusting how you've seen your people pleasing, you're naturally going to be looking for people who seem to have gotten the download on the healthy kind. And, understandably, you're likely going to look for the actions in their lives. You could be drawn to copying their behaviors. You might even consider signing up for the types of volunteering they do or joining the organizations they are a part of. As you watch and learn, you could be tempted to give out some little "baby coughs" of activities because it's what the "grown-ups" are doing.

While I do think learning from the lives of others is important, I want to caution you from trying to take on the template of someone else's life, of someone else's assignment from God, and shoehorning it into your own. I want you to see God's purpose for your life; I don't want you to rely on trying to live through someone else's. Jesus has offered you a redeemed understanding of people pleasing, one in which you act out of genuine love rather than what you can extract from a person or a situation. Yes, learn from others who model this well. But my desire is for you to know the Lord for yourself, to know that you can approach Him without having to go through someone else, without having to act like someone else.

This beautiful antivenom of heartfelt, unselfish, God-led people pleasing isn't complicated. It doesn't require strategy. It's not buried or mysterious. Every day there are people who need to experience the love of God—at your grocery store, at work, at your kid's soccer practice. When you stop seeing them as people to meet your needs for approval and attention, everything changes. It takes back what that snake of old from the garden distorted—our need for each other—and returns it to us renewed and healthy.

As Jesus said, "I was hungry and you gave me food, I was thirsty and you gave me drink, I was a stranger and you welcomed me, I was naked and you clothed me, I was sick and you visited me, I was in prison and you came to me. . . . Truly, I say to you, as you did it to one of the least of these my brothers, you did it to me" (Matthew 25:35–40).

Let's Chat About It

I know it can feel counterintuitive to move into a new season of people pleasing when you're trying to leave the trap of people pleasing. But I believe you can see how the beautiful parts of caring and serving others haven't been the problem; it's been the heart behind it.

1. What are your thoughts on people pleasing from a healthy place?
2. Is there something about it that makes you a little nervous? What is that, and why?
3. What is an experience you've had where the thing you needed to help you get better was also the very thing you were trying to avoid or get away from? What happened?

Here's a prayer for us as we enter a fresh season of loving and serving others well and from the right heart:

God, You show me over and over in Your Word that I will have joy and satisfaction when I love others well, when I bless others with no thought of what I'm getting in the bargain. Help me serve from that place. Give me supernatural joy. Guide me in what You would have me do. In my serving, let me also honor my family and work, children and spouse, well. Thank You for the incredible privilege to be part of a community in which I bless others, others bless me, and together, we fulfill Your design. In Jesus' name, amen.

Chapter 11

IT'S JUST US NOW

HOW HARD COULD IT BE?

I looked at all the parts and pieces that had been delivered, then glanced again at the instruction manual. I stood, electric drill in hand, piles of stained wood laid in semiorganized stacks across the back porch. *How would Jana the DIY Closet Project Queen tackle this?* I thought. *Maybe I should wait for Jeremy.* But he was going to be attending to a series of obligations throughout a heavy workday, and I really wanted to get started.

And that, my friend, was how I began the project of building my girls a playset in the backyard. And when I say playset, I mean the swings, the slide, the fort, the whole thing.

I started by putting together the ladder. Easy peasy. Then I worked on a base piece. Nailed it. As the hot afternoon wore on, more and more boards came together.

Now, the instruction manual was very clear that several of the steps required two people. But I was so in the zone, so determined to prove that I could do it on my own, that I came up with all kinds of workarounds and hacks. I leaned certain pieces up against the house to continue the construction. I dragged heavy panels across the yard. Jeremy arrived home at dinnertime and was encouraging of my progress, but a little surprised. After all, this was a project he thought we were going to be doing together. But I wanted to get it done for our daughter's birthday, and daylight was burning. I worked into the night.

The next day, there she was, the Good Ship Vuolo Playground. And yes, I was very proud of myself. Sure, my back hurt for the next few days. And, sure, the playground had a slight sway to it. But I had done it, all by myself.

Ta-da!

Except that Jeremy needed to circle back to the playground within a couple of weeks and anchor it more deeply to the ground. I had done as good a job as I could have on it, with the strength I had; but to make it a little more secure, a little surer, I needed to have the strength of others to come alongside me to make the structure sound.

I don't tell you this to diminish the work I put into this project; believe me, I'm pretty proud of myself. The girls love to play in their little backyard playground under the bright California sky, and I love to be out there with them, a happy satisfaction filling my heart that I could do this for them. What I am saying is that it can be tempting to try to do something solo that would be best achieved with help by your side. An extra helping of strength comes when we don't try to take on the big project of healing and freedom in our life all by ourselves.

There's a beautiful book in the Old Testament called Ecclesiastes. In that book, the preacher reflected on his life and shared what he had learned. He talked about all the study he had done, exploring all kinds of knowledge and facts. He recounted the building projects he'd accomplished throughout his life. He talked about the wealth he had acquired, the pleasure he'd run after, the entertainment he'd engaged in.

And what did he discover? So much of what he'd chased and worried over and worked for didn't have much meaning at the end of the day. And then he shared the things that do matter in the course of a human life, including our relationships with others.

He wrote,

Two are better than one, because they have a good reward for their toil. For if they fall, one will lift up his fellow. But woe to him who is alone when he falls and has not another to lift him up! Again, if two lie together, they keep warm, but how can one keep warm alone? And though a man might prevail against one who is alone, two will withstand him—a threefold cord is not quickly broken. (Ecclesiastes 4:9–12)

You may be tempted to think that you can move forward in healing from your unhealthy people-pleasing ways all on your own. You've got the information about the antivenom solution, where we talked about healing from people pleasing by pleasing people for all the right reasons and motives, serving others simply from the unencumbered joy of serving. *I've got it*, you think. *I can put this whole new life together on my own. I don't need any help! I'll just put my new motives and approaches together and drag it out into the yard of life, ready for action!* And listen, I have no doubt that you can make a lot of progress on your own. But it's a tender thing to learn how to serve and love people the way Jesus does, without flinching, posturing, extracting, and calculating what you can get from others when that has been your way of life.

Again, your way of unhealthy people pleasing has a flavor to it that's unique to you, just as mine does for me. We ended up in the snare of people pleasing for a variety of reasons. The ways we move to a healthy form of serving others will look different for each of us. But I believe there is one foundational truth for all of us: you have to let others in, and that begins with having a relationship with Jesus.

What does it look like to have a relationship with Jesus? Well, it begins with something that we're not always so great at. We like to talk about knowing Jesus, the gentle Shepherd, the radical Rabbi, the Messiah who turned a culture on its head. And He is all of that. But knowing *about* Him versus actually knowing Him (and Him knowing you) are different things.

I realize that a whole variety of people are going to pick up this book, some of whom would say they already have a relationship with Jesus, some of whom are curious about what that means and what that would look like, some who feel like they got burned by religion or religious people, and some who are hearing about Jesus for the first time.

Friend, wherever you are in that experience, consider Jesus. He was not just a nice teacher who said some interesting and insightful things. He claimed to be God Himself and the only one who can save us from our sin. When Jesus entered this world as a man, He did remarkable things. He performed miracles, fed the hungry, healed the sick, and loved the unlovable. He was the most gentle, kind, and gracious man anyone had ever met. But still, people hated Him to the point that they crucified Him on a cross. Why? Because He told us that we are sinners and that we need to turn from our sin and follow Him. That message of repentance and faith was too much for so many, so they rejected him. But even still, Jesus invites anyone who would come to Him to receive Him as their Lord and Savior.

His invitation is gracious and clear: "Come to me, all who labor and are heavy laden, and I will give you rest. Take my yoke upon you, and learn from me, for I am gentle and lowly in heart, and you will find rest for your souls. For my yoke is easy, and my burden is light" (Matthew 11:28–30).

You don't have to have a certain level of Bible knowledge or a profound grasp of theology; all of that can come later. What I think you do know is that you've been struggling. You've been trying to figure out all this people-pleasing stuff on your own. You've tried to make yourself feel safe, feel seen, feel known by all your efforts, and it's left you feeling even more scared, more invisible, and more misunderstood.

Jesus offers you a real peace. Jesus sees you. Jesus knows you. He loves you so much that He came to rescue you from your sin. On the cross, Jesus took the payment for the sins of all who would put their trust in Him.

And now, you can know Him—not just about Him but *Him*, His mercy, His grace, and His compassion for you. Put your faith in Jesus.

That's what it means to be a Christian: to follow Jesus as your Lord and Savior.

Now, am I saying that as a Christian, you will never struggle with people pleasing from the wrong motives again? No. It's something you and I will deal with, something we'll need to keep a close eye on. The paths we have taken over and over make it all too easy to go down those paths again and again. But Jesus offers us a new way to live, a new way to think. And He walks with us, tugging at our hearts when we veer toward dangerous lanes.

The disciple who was Jesus' closest friend, John, wrote about how to experience having the darkness of our sin lifted from our lives. In one of the last letters John wrote, he said,

God is light, and in him is no darkness at all. If we say we have fellowship with him while we walk in darkness, we lie and do not practice the truth. But if we walk in the light, as he is in the light, we have fellowship with one another, and the blood of Jesus his Son cleanses us from all sin. If we say we have no sin, we deceive ourselves, and the truth is not in us. If we confess our sins, he is faithful and just to forgive us our sins and to cleanse us from all unrighteousness. (1 John 1:5–9)

Am I suggesting that you come to Jesus for what you can get out of it? After all, we bring our nothing and He gives us eternity. We experience a peace that this world cannot give us. We come with our suitcases of sin and He gives us forgiveness. But don't miss this: following Jesus also means that we live like He did. He loved us with such an incredible love that, in return, we gladly leave aside our selfish motives and pursuits. It means we are free to love and serve others with a heart that isn't seeking for anything else. We receive an incredible inheritance when we follow Jesus, and in response, we love others the way He does, with sacrificial and contented hearts.

Take a minute. Think about all of this. And then, if you're ready, no matter the background you've had, wherever you would categorize your spiritual experiences up to today, pray and ask the Lord to forgive you for your sin and to rescue you from it. Confess your sins to Him. Put your faith in Jesus to save you. And find the beautiful peace and rest that He promises.

———

I know we talked about how the word *sin* isn't exactly fashionable today. Here's another one you don't hear much about: *confession*.

See, to be able to take steps of freedom, we have to acknowledge what we're walking away from, and the grip it has had on us. For me, that first step was confessing to God that I had made an idol out of other people's opinions. I had worshiped at that idol with my time, my thoughts, my behavior, and what could really qualify as devotion, the amount of effort I gave to it. When I could finally see my people pleasing as the sin it was, and then come clean with God about that sin, I truly turned to Jesus to help me face and deal with it.

I know it can sound really scary to take that kind of a step, to be that vulnerable at the spiritual level, and to confess it to God. But with the same grace and mercy Jesus showed the woman caught in adultery we talked about in chapter 6, He doesn't condemn you. You have the opportunity through Him to go and leave your life of sin. Air out your soul and let a little light in.

Here's something else that has really helped me. Once I made that confession to God, once I acknowledged the sin that had been consuming my life through trying to live by other people's opinions, I needed to open up to a few trusted people around me. This struggle I had been keeping secret, this burden that had isolated me and held power over me, when I began to talk about it with others, when I pulled it out into the light, that drained its tanks.

You might find it harder to confess to others what's been going on with you than it is to talk to God about it. Why is that? Because it's one thing to talk to God about it privately. You know that He's going to be kind, compassionate, and forgiving. But other people? The people you've been trying to impress, the people for whom you have built this whole complicated facade of behaviors and avoidance and isolation and performance?

You just can't guarantee how they might respond when you start pulling it all down.

And that's scary.

But think about it for a minute. Let's say that I was determined to keep my girls' playground a solo endeavor. I might have been able to keep it up for a while. But at the first bluster of the Santa Ana winds we get through here, the whole thing could have toppled. Even if the winds had stayed at bay, just through the regular playtime use of the playground, those screws and bolts that I had only been able to tighten according to my own strength would have continued to loosen and loosen until, one day, things would have started to come apart. To make a change, it's going to take a team. To reinforce what you're building with God. To point out the weak spots in the construction.

In bringing up the topic of confession, I have to tell you that I feel a heavy responsibility to explain to you as clearly as possible what it is and what it isn't. As I wrote in *Becoming Free Indeed*, I suffered for a long time under a style of confession that was anything but life-giving and biblical. Growing up under the teachings of Bill Gothard, I was taught that confession was the necessary ingredient on my part to keep God from severely punishing me or striking me dead. If I forgot any line item, if I left out any detail, I was putting myself in absolute peril. It was a superstition, with all the responsibility on me to keep God from taking me out. And I was expected to confess any assumed infraction to the hundreds and hundreds of rules under that system, to go to my mom and dad, who were considered my "authority," not to process my struggles with anyone else. For example, if I noticed a boy, I would "confess" it. It never crossed my mind that I could process a normal crush on a cute boy with my sisters, with my best friend. I lived in the weird tension of trying to present my life and my behaviors as perfectly as possible while also constantly scanning myself for any and everything to confess about.

I can assure you, that kind of confession keeps you on a wild, twisting roller coaster of the sickliest kind of people pleasing.

The right kind of confession I'm talking about is one where we're honest with each other about what we're struggling with; where we know, according to Scripture, that we've sinned; and we process where we're trying to grow in our walk with God. It's not some kind of magic spell for containing God like an angry genie in a bottle. It's not a tool for shame but rather a relief and a joy to share our humanness with others and to experience the grace God brings when we're honest and open.

I think it would be so helpful for you to have two or three people you can trust, people you can have accountability with, people you are on the same page with in your walk with God and who want to see you be able to serve and love people in the best way possible.

These are your long-haul kind of people. There will be the moment when you initially confess your sin of selfish people pleasing, and there will be the moments after, when you need to be able to talk about where you're struggling, when the temptations of people pleasing from the wrong posture crop up.

Okay, Jing, you might be thinking. *Where am I supposed to find people like that?*

I'm not going to pretend like just anyone you might encounter in a church would have the maturity to come alongside you with the right balance of encouragement and exhortation. But it's the best place I know to start looking. Look, none of us has it all together. None of us has it all figured out. But people who are also committed to growing, to refining their walk with God, who love others well and from the right motives, those are the ones you're looking for. Jeremy has been that for me in this journey. I also have a woman in my life who is older than me who knows of my struggles and has been such a powerful mentor. She and her husband go to church with Jeremy and me, and her love, example, support, and wisdom have been so life-giving.

That brings me to another important point. When I talk about confessing and processing with a few trusted people, being on the same page about the goal is so important. It feels good to have someone in your court saying, "That's right, girl! Don't you let so-and-so talk to you like that!" and "Be a boss, girl! Demand what you want and need, and don't take anything less!" But as you and I know, that approach to life is only a temporary fix.

———

During the days Jeremy and I were living in Texas, something struck fear into the hearts of homeowners across parts of the state. While this issue can happen across the country, Texas is at the top of the list for a phenomenon known as black mold. Black mold begins in a house in a number of ways, from having windows that aren't sealed properly to small leaks that go undetected for a long time. Homes built for energy conservation often have issues because they're so well-constructed against the wide range of elements. Texas has wild weather, from the searing heat of the summer to the icy cold of winter, which also means that moisture trapped inside the houses built to withstand all that has a hard time getting out.

Unfortunately, once black mold takes hold in a house, it can spread quickly and cause lots of health issues for the people who live there. Would it be great if you could just paint over any black mold that started to show up on your walls? Sure. Covering up that nasty stuff, even thinking to yourself that you're effectively sealing it off, sure seems a lot more convenient and less expensive.

But the core issue hasn't been resolved. When you see a house with a mold problem, it's wild. In the areas where the black mold has taken hold, they have to take that room down to the studs. And then they have to treat the studs! It's an involved, expensive, significant process that requires making sure you've identified all the areas where there is mold and then carefully removing those areas that have been touched.

When you invite people into your life to help you recover from your people-pleasing ways, it could feel really good to populate that group with people who only tell you all kinds of meme-worthy, ego-building affirmations and confuse it for encouragement. But you and I are trying to remove the black mold of people pleasing from the home of our hearts. We've acknowledged that its presence has made us sick and has us behaving in self-centric ways. We don't need people to help us come paint over the mess; we need people who help us take things all the way back to the studs and help us rebuild how we see loving and serving others. We need people who take seriously the sickness of heart we've experienced through our behavior.

That's why I want to encourage you to make sure you're inviting people into this process who understand that you want to be a healthy people pleaser, meaning that you want to help and engage others based on what you have to give through your relationship with Christ, not based on what you can get. Should your "team" also encourage you to make sure you're operating in a healthy balance, with the appropriate focus given to your marriage and kids and your health? Of course. And they'll also be there to exhort you when you need to push yourself a bit.

That's another word you might not hear too often today—*exhort*. We mainly like to talk about encouraging each other, which is a beautiful thing. Sometimes we even think that encouraging and exhorting are the same thing. If you look it up in one of our modern dictionaries, you'll see it right there, *exhorting* defined as encouragement. But when you wind back the clock to the time of the writing of the New Testament of the Bible, to exhort meant something different. The Greek word for exhorting means to admonish.[1] That's a very different thing than our typical way of encouraging each other. We tend to think of encouraging as getting people pumped up, telling them they can do it, telling them how great they are. To admonish means you're advising someone, maybe in a way they would rather not hear. You're challenging them to come up higher. You're warning them when you see them getting a little sloppy.

I don't think we're too good at this original meaning of exhorting today. We're either talking to people on a bubbly surface level—*you're great, you're great, everything is great!*—or we're chopping people off at the knees, posting horribly harsh responses on social media and in emails, cutting people to the quick with our criticism and comments.

But that life-giving thing called exhortation?

It's like we've never heard of it, and we don't know how to do it.

Let me show you a place in Scripture that carries this distinction of exhorting and encouragement. The apostle Paul and his friend Silas spent some time in a city called Thessalonica in Greece. It's a little over three hundred miles from the capital city of Athens. They went there to tell people about Jesus, and for three weeks, they taught and talked at the synagogue. At first, things seemed to be going well, but then some people became jealous and angry at their message about Jesus. Paul and Silas escaped to a friend's house when this group came after them, then had to take off during the dark of the night to head out of town. A few months later, Paul wrote his first letter to the people who had come to believe in Jesus in Thessalonica.

In that letter, Paul wanted to do a couple of things. He wanted to make sure the believers in Thessalonica knew how much he cared about them and how important they were as an example to others. And he also wanted them to stay aware and vigilant to live their lives according to what they had come to believe. His letter was a reminder of the things he talked to them about when he was with them a few months earlier. He wrote, "We exhorted each one of you and encouraged you and charged you to walk in a manner worthy of God, who calls you into his own kingdom and glory" (1 Thessalonians 2:12).

Do you see it? Paul used that word *exhort*. He reminded the Thessalonians that he and Silas advised them when they needed it, corrected them when they needed it, cheered them on when they needed it, and gave them the assignment to walk in a God-honoring way. Those are all related *and* different things.

I think it's really important to make the distinction for you and me when it comes to having the right people alongside us in our journeys. We need people who have the courage and the permission from us to raise a red flag when we're headed for the ditch. We need people who take us just as seriously as we do the toxicity of the moldy people pleasing that has been sliming the walls of our hearts. We need people who know how to do that with love, care, authenticity, and honesty.

A vibrant, healthy church based on the grace of Jesus and on His Word in Scripture has people who will be honored to take part in this next chapter of your life. They will hold your confessions, your challenges, your joys, and your struggles with confidentiality and care. They will check in on you. They'll tell you some tough things you need to hear, and they'll cheer you on. They'll be a real-time example of the right kind of people pleasing, and you'll learn so much from walking through life with them.

———

When Jeremy and I got ready to buy our home here in California, it was a bit of a blur. As I mentioned, we'd been living in a home close to the seminary where Jeremy was working on his doctorate degree. It was a great place and we were happy to be there. One day, our friends saw a house come on the market that they thought would be perfect for us. We weren't really in the market, but they were so enthusiastic about the place, we thought we'd go take a look, just out of curiosity.

We made the twenty-minute drive out to the foothills of the San Gabriel mountains.

And from the minute we walked in the front door, we just knew. This was home.

The style of the house was exactly us. The layout was just what we wanted, a place we could host our friends and family. The backyard gave us a beautiful view of the foothills. As we walked through each room, it just kept ticking all the boxes. I know you're not supposed to show a lot of excitement when you go to buy a car or a house; for negotiating, it's best not to show all your cards. But I've got to say, Jeremy and I both were struggling not to burst out and exclaim, "We'll take it!"

By the time we finished the house tour, we could already fully picture our lives there. But there was a really important thing we had to do before we signed off on the sales contract. And that was having a house inspector come look at the property.

Our house inspector was great. Thorough and knowledgeable.

While thankfully he didn't find any major issues with the house, he was able to identify a few things that we needed to make sure were part of the contract, a handful of things that needed to be repaired or replaced before we purchased the home. He was the one who pointed out that there was no attic access, something I wouldn't have noticed until we'd moved in and I was looking to put our Christmas decorations away. As it turns out, attic access is an important thing, and not just for storage. It's how you're able to get to certain systems for repair, how you can check on the roof, how you insulate the house. We were grateful for his expertise and guidance as we walked through the process. While we had some knowledge about issues we should look out for, while we had friends who had already walked through the home-buying process and had some great advice for us, calling in a professional to look at everything through his practiced eye was invaluable.

While I absolutely want to encourage you to build a community around yourself, while I want you to find a trusted inner circle of people you can process with, who will encourage and exhort you, you may want to consider bringing in a professional. Because the tentacles of unhealthy people pleasing can run so deep, someone who knows how to do a thorough inspection and has the professional tools to help you make repairs can be absolute gold. I am so thankful for the skilled Christian counselor who has helped me overcome the specific issues I have faced in my own people pleasing. This person, who has the education, gifting, and expertise to take a professional look at the "home" I'm building for a healthier chapter in my life, has been priceless in showing me what healthy versus unhealthy people pleasing looks like. They've helped me gain "attic access," allowing me to now be able to pull some things out of emotional storage to sort through, giving me a view of what hangs over my head. They provide insight into why I struggle in some of the ways I do. They are a source of information and approaches that make the path I am walking more solid.

Just like the community you're discovering, just like the trusted friends you're opening up to, use wisdom when searching for the right professional. If you visit with them a couple of times and it's not the right fit, try someone else. Specifically, look for someone whose starting point is the Bible and who has professional experience in helping people with unhealthy behavior patterns of approval seeking. Look, not all counselors are the same; you'll need to put in some homework. But I'm telling you, it's worth it. If I didn't think so, I wouldn't talk about it here, for everyone to see. Get that internal house inspector involved and let their ability and experience be an important part of your growth.

Whew.

This was a lot, wasn't it? It feels super vulnerable to let others in, to talk with them about some of the things that can feel the least flattering in our lives, this misplaced desire to have others' approval. It's not necessarily a fun thing to invite others into the process, but it is so good. It is so healing. And I want to remind you again that it all begins with Jesus occupying that primary place in the home of your heart. All these other people you're bringing in? They're awesome. You were made to need their kind of love and support and joy in your life. But Jesus needs to be first. He is the one who loves you best.

He is the one who leads you home.

Let's Chat About It

There are things in life that we need to tackle, but it can be all too tempting to minimize or underestimate those things. People pleasing is one of them. Seeing our selfish motives in our people pleasing as sin can be a hard pill to swallow. To consider getting help with our people-pleasing challenges can feel like a relief, but it can also feel incredibly scary.

1. Do you feel ready to see your unhealthy people-pleasing ways as sinful? Why or why not?
2. On a scale of one to ten, with one meaning that you feel good about it and ten meaning that it sounds completely overwhelming and terrifying, where would you say you are in terms of talking with a trusted, mature friend about your people-pleasing behaviors and motives?
3. What would you be free from if you could talk about your challenges with people pleasing, could get the help you need to overcome old patterns, and could have accountability within your community?

Friend, while I think we covered many important things in this chapter, the most important one is having Jesus in your life as your Savior. My prayer is that you would put your trust in Him and find the freedom and joy only He can give.

Chapter 12

YOURS TO GIVE

SO HERE WE ARE. WE'VE TAKEN A TRIP DOWN TO THE
very core of our hearts to understand why we've been too controlled
by the opinions and approval of other people. We've discovered
the ways that trying to please people from an unhealthy place has
shown up in our lives and what it's cost us. We've considered a different way of looking at our relationships with others, how to still
care about people, to still have them as a needed and beloved community in our lives, but without performing and pretending from
selfish motives. You've heard me talk a lot about my relationship
with God and how that has been the most important component of
my own journey in people pleasing. He is the one who has guided
me, loved me, and set me free.

Wherever you are today as we bring our journey to a close,
wherever you are in your relationship with God, it's my sincere

prayer that you will continue to grow in your relationships with others and with Him. I truly believe that the only way we find healing and wholeness when we've had the bondage of unhealthy people pleasing in our lives is through the grace of God, by bringing our lives to Him and letting Him guide us into a better way of living. I pray your heart remains open and listening for His voice.

I want us to spend this remaining time taking a deeper look at how you and I can enjoy loving and giving, just like Jesus. And when I say "enjoy," I mean it. All the ways I used to try to people please were not what I would call enjoyable. People pleasing seemed necessary and stressful and anxiety-inducing. It often seemed like a chore, something I *had* to do in order to gain favor or stay out of trouble with someone. When I began to understand all the ways I was using pleasing to extract from others, and when I began laying down my motives and my hunger for approval, I became free to serve in a more genuine way. Once that happened, I realized something surprising: I was really enjoying loving and serving others, simply to bless them. I didn't know for a long time that God's expectation that we will take care of one another could be so fun, could leave me so content.

It's an experience I would love for you to have as well.

So where do we begin? What are some practical ways we can begin to experience this healthy, right, life-giving kind of people pleasing?

I get so excited thinking about this because when you belong to Jesus, He does something so unique for you. Through the Holy Spirit, you are specifically gifted to help others in particular ways. Now, if you don't yet have a relationship with Jesus, you might think I'm talking about a talent you have. Your talent is a beautiful thing, and I do encourage you to use it to help others. But this gifting I'm talking about is something different, something intentionally provided to a believer that makes them part of a bigger whole.

Before Jesus ascended back to heaven after His resurrection, He let His disciples and followers know that they would be receiving the Holy Spirit (John 14–16). As part of having the Holy Spirit come into their lives, they would receive specific gifts, a supernatural ability with which to serve their families and communities. Here are two passages of Scripture that talk about how the Holy Spirit empowers the Christian life:

> To each is given the manifestation of the Spirit for the common good. For to one is given through the Spirit the utterance of wisdom, and to another the utterance of knowledge according to the same Spirit, to another faith by the same Spirit, to another gifts of healing by the one Spirit, to another the working of miracles, to another prophecy, to another the ability to distinguish between spirits, to another various kinds of tongues, to another the interpretation of tongues. All these are empowered by one and the same Spirit, who apportions to each one individually as he wills. (1 Corinthians 12:7–11)

> As in one body we have many members, and the members do not all have the same function, so we, though many, are one body in Christ, and individually members one of another. Having gifts that differ according to the grace given to us, let us use them: if prophecy, in proportion to our faith; if service, in our serving; the one who teaches, in his teaching; the one who exhorts, in his exhortation; the one who contributes, in generosity; the one who leads, with zeal; the one who does acts of mercy, with cheerfulness. (Romans 12:4–8)

I realize that was a whole lot of scripture to get through, but I know it's worth it. I hope you picked up on all the different gifts God gives, and that each person has the gifts they do for distinct reasons. Not only do you have the talents you were naturally graced with, but when you belong to Jesus, you also have this incredible spiritual gift available to serve others with. You don't have to compare yourself to anyone else, because God didn't design you to be anyone else; He has a distinct calling and gift for you.

I think God has given Jeremy and me both a spiritual gift of hospitality. It was one of the early things we talked about in our relationship, as we were dating and expressing what priorities we had and what kind of life we prayed to build. To this day, we both delight in hosting, in having over friends and our small group and other types of gatherings. Here's something really important I want you to see. Do you remember what would get my unhealthy people pleasing churned up into an absolute internal, emotional storm in my early marriage? Yep, hosting. Being hospitable. Something that I do believe God gave me a gift for.

So why do you suppose it was an area that became a battleground for me?

We have a real Enemy who doesn't want us to walk in the life Jesus came to give us. He's been deceiving us since the garden, and he's still at it. Just like the Enemy warped our need for one another into something twisted that has kept you and me captive to approval seeking and conflict avoiding, he'll also do his best to keep you from using your unique gifts for the benefit of your family and friends and church. It's no mistake that one of the very areas God had gifted me to serve was also the very area that caused me so much stress, to the point I just shut down. I didn't see the schemes of the Enemy as clearly back then. But now, now that I understand how people pleasing can either be used to tear us up or for us to build up others, I'm getting a whole lot wiser to the Enemy's tricks.

One of Jesus' close friends and disciples, Peter, reminded us, "Be sober-minded; be watchful. Your adversary the devil prowls around like a roaring lion, seeking someone to devour" (1 Peter 5:8). You might find that you struggle the most with unhealthy people pleasing right in the middle of something you feel God-gifted to do, to the point that you want to quit. But Peter also encourageed us to remember, "His [Jesus'] divine power has granted to us all things that pertain to life and godliness, through the knowledge of him who called us to his own glory and excellence" (2 Peter 1:3).

There's another trick we can fall for when it comes to using our gifts in service to others. It's when you feel like you don't really matter that much in the grand scheme of things, that your contributions won't make much of a difference. Maybe you feel there are already plenty of people involved in your family and in your church to make sure things are covered. Maybe you feel like your gift isn't all that special or important. If that's you, I get it. I spent a long time loving being part of a church family but not thinking I really had anything to add. But there's a beautiful mystery about being a part of God's family that I want you to know about. We're more than just a group that meets consistently. We're a body. And a body exists and is sustained by all the parts working together.

———

When it comes to the way our body operates, those parts and functions that we might overlook, not know about, or not see as all that important can actually be some of the most important of all. Jeremy and I have been reflecting on a word recently when it comes to this: *indispensable.*

Because God intends the church to function as a body, we have to understand that each of us is indispensable. You are indispensable. The body simply won't function the same way without you. God gave you a gift that the body needs, and it's yours to give.

No matter how insignificant you might sometimes feel, no matter how often you might be tempted to compare your gift and what you have to offer up against someone else's gifting, you matter. The apostle Paul said it this way: "On the contrary, the parts of the body that seem to be weaker are indispensable" (1 Corinthians 12:22).

I don't know what your history is with being part of a church community. Whether you were raised going to church or not, I want to ask you to lay aside whatever those experiences are and lean in for a few minutes.

Friend, when you are walking with Jesus, when you have His Holy Spirit living inside you, you have something so important that is yours to give. And it's not just that your gift would be a nice thing to have around; Paul said it's indispensable.

Think about a church service. So often we focus on the people serving in the more public moments. The worship leader. The person who gives communion thoughts. The pastor. Are these all important roles? For sure. In many ways, those who serve with those kinds of gifts are like the powerful parts of the anatomy of the church body. Even if you think your gift and your presence in a church is insignificant or unnecessary, can I lovingly tell you you're wrong? You're indispensable! You're important to the kingdom of God.

That's why I want to encourage you to make sure you're part of a healthy, Bible-believing, vibrant, grace-filled church community. Do I believe that you can receive remarkable healing from your people-pleasing past just between you and Jesus? Of course. But out of gratitude for that experience and for the important part that you are in the body of Christ, the church, please don't miss this: You are needed. And you were created for this.

———

Maybe you feel like you don't know yet what special gifts God has given you. That's all right; He is always available for you to ask. I would tell you to start there, to pray for God to show you. Also, dive into God's Word, learning more about what spiritual gifts are and how they are used to serve others. May I give a quick piece of advice on this? Choose an area to serve at your church and see how it goes. You may find you excel in one area but not so much in another. You

You are needed. And you were created for this.

can also ask trusted friends and family where they see God at work in you.

It's not been my intention in this chapter to give you a full run-down on every kind of way to serve God and others. I don't really believe in those "spiritual gift tests" that people tend to give. I'm confident you can explore this further with your church, your spouse, and your trusted friends. The main idea I want you to carry from here is how needed you are to the people you are doing life with.

As you grow into deeper relationships, into more authentic connection with your people, you won't just see the scales of unhealthy people pleasing start to fall away. You'll also have an assurance, a confidence in your life, in who God created you to be. Because you and I have struggled in the past, this fresh sense of tenacity and calm and sureness might feel a little surprising. *What is this new feeling?* you might wonder. You might even second-guess yourself a bit; after all, you spent a long time beating yourself up and feeling pretty crummy about yourself. So this new flavor of happiness and contentedness just might be a little confusing.

Guess what? It's simply the evidence that you are now walking in the way God intended. Paul reminded us, "God gave us a spirit not of fear but of power and love and self-control" (2 Timothy 1:7). How amazing is that, that when we have the Holy Spirit in our hearts, we have strength? We can love well. And we can exercise the self-discipline to keep our people pleasing on the healthy side of the scale. For far too long, I walked afraid, completely at the whim of my ever-changing emotions, resentful and bitter of the very people I was trying to impress. Even though I had heard of God my whole life, even though I was trying to follow Him, I didn't understand the power that comes through receiving His grace. When I finally exchanged all my efforts for His mercy and salvation, my heaviness of heart lifted.

Let me be clear: I still have tough days. I sometimes can feel myself slip back into a people-pleasing pattern in which I'm shielding and protecting myself. It's my guess that I'll always have to keep an eye on it. But what I know now is that my flaws and imperfections do not disqualify me from being loved by God. They don't keep me from offering what I have to give to others. Like the apostle Paul wrote, "Not that I have already obtained this or am already perfect, but I press on to make it my own, because Christ Jesus has made me his own" (Philippians 3:12). The same is true for you, my friend. You are a light, even if you have a few shadows too.

———

She really was at the end of her rope. She felt like she'd given all she had to give. Her husband was gone. Her little boy was frail with hunger. She had been so desperate to find a solution, but she'd given up.

She lived in a town called Zarephath. When times were good, it was a port city with a busy, vibrant harbor, people from faraway places sailing into the village. But famine had struck the area, and there was nothing to eat, nothing to forage for.

She was gathering sticks to make a small fire when the stranger approached her. He asked for water, which she got for him. Then he asked for something to eat. That was something she didn't think she had to give. She told him that she only had a small bit of flour and oil left, that she was actually gathering sticks to build a small fire over which to bake the last of what she had. So dire was her situation that she told the stranger that this was her last act, that she would make this meager meal for her and her son, and then they would die.

But the stranger was insistent. He told her that God knew of her desperate situation but that she needed to give him a morsel of the bread she was about to make, then feed her son and herself, and that God would see to it that her jug of oil and her jar of flour would not run out.

I look at the story of the widow and her encounter with one of

But what I know now is that my flaws and imperfections do not disqualify me from being loved by God.

God's prophets, Elijah, in the book of 1 Kings in the Old Testament with amazement. Here was someone who was at the end of her rope. I would have totally understood if she had told this stranger, this prophet Elijah, that she had nothing left to give, nothing to spare, and that she certainly wasn't going to give him the tiny dusting of flour and drops of oil she had scraped together.

But in that moment, she believed in something bigger than her fatigue, her confusion, her desperate neediness. She believed that maybe, just maybe, God could show up to do what she could not.

So she did it. She made a small cake of the remnants of her flour and oil. She then served it to Elijah. "And she and he and her household ate for many days," Scripture says in 1 Kings chapter 17. "The jar of flour was not spent, neither did the jug of oil become empty, according to the word of the LORD that he spoke by Elijah" (vv. 15–16).

What Elijah knew that she did not when their encounter began was that God had sent Elijah specifically to this woman, to make this request for this insufficient and wildly precious bit of bread. Her solution came through her serving, giving what she had and trusting God with the rest. She gave what she had to give.

And God did the rest.

As you begin to walk into a healthier way of viewing being in community and the contributions you make there, I want you to know this: you don't have to *make* it all happen. You do have responsibilities as part of the body of Christ. But the results of your giving are not all on you. God simply asks us to bring what we have, and He provides. I see this so many places in Scripture, from the story I was just telling you, all the way into the New Testament and Jesus' ministry. You've probably heard about the time Jesus was able to multiply the simple lunch of the five loaves of bread and two fish of a young boy in the crowd. Through the generosity of that boy, Jesus did the rest, turning a small meal for one into a feast for five thousand (Matthew 14:13–21).

I remind you of this because sometimes, even when we're operating in the spiritual gifts God gives us, we can begin to take on burdens that aren't meant for us. While you absolutely are indispensable in the family of God, I would never want you to think that you are the one who has to figure out how to somehow do the miraculous. I've seen people move away from unhealthy people pleasing into a place of healthy people pleasing, only to get caught up again in an unhealthy pattern because they won't rest. They won't rely on letting God do what only He can do. Can we go a little further, push a little harder, go an extra mile? Yes, and we should; God can give us that extra ability. Does that mean that we can *will* the outcome to happen the way we think it should, that by our efforts we can manipulate the hand of God?

No.

There's something so freeing about giving what you have to give and then watching what God will do. Your gifts are meant to help and serve others, not to craft a path to accomplish what you think would be best or to use for self-serving means. I only mention this caution because I think it's important as you determine what church you're called to be a part of. If someone is teaching that spiritual gifts are a way for you to build the future you want, for you to push God into catering to your agenda, I'd say to keep looking. A healthy church understands and puts into practice that our God is all-powerful and that He holds our future.

CONCLUSION

WE RECENTLY HAD A BIG GROUP OF FRIENDS OVER, hosting a fun night where all the kids played and we drifted back and forth from conversations in the house and around the kitchen island out to the patio while the kids swarmed the play fort and we fired up the pizza oven.

And I have to share with you: I was able to host and refill drinks and hustle around the kitchen with joy.

Complete joy.

The floors got crunchy with crumbs. The girls' toys were scattered all across the house. The throw pillows on the couch got squished. There were some spills and messes and a skinned knee or two. I didn't know a reference made to a movie. It was a night of chaos and community.

And I felt like I was there, truly there, not standing outside of it all, wringing my hands at what my guests might be thinking, taking inventory of all the places I was coming up short. No, by God's grace, I was joyfully present, enjoying having my friends over, serving them with the gifts God's given me to give. As the California sun set in a blaze of crimson, orange, and pink, and the night air began to cool, contentment and a profound sense of freedom filled my heart.

Did we make some tasty food that night? Yes, we did. But nothing on that menu tasted as good as the freedom I experienced. All the little moments that have tripped me up in the past were present and accounted for, everything from a messy house to being a little behind on cultural references. There was a time when this may have sent me reeling into a spiral of isolation.

But loving people for who they are and for how I can genuinely bless them has set me free. Being loved by a husband who has pushed me to speak my opinions and has embraced my awkwardness and goofiness has set me free. Getting myself off my mind so much has set me free. Writing books about my experiences in a dangerous religious system and my battle with people pleasing has set me free. At times, those freedoms have been fought for. There have been times of tears and doubts and a temptation to repeat old patterns. But God has never left me alone in my freedom fight.

Friend, He's fighting for you too. And when you ask Him to be with you, He will. When you ask Him to help you, He will.

I've given you what I can on this people-pleasing thing that has kept you and me snared for so long. I hope that in giving you my story, it helps you. That it makes you feel not as alone. That you are learning, just like I am, that we are loved as we are, that we are accepted by a gracious God. I've given what I have to give, in all its imperfections and shortcomings. I'm humbled that you've received it.

And now I'm ready to see what God is going to do in your life. If you have put your faith in Jesus, you can be at peace knowing that it is well with your soul. When God sent His Son to us, the angels said, "Glory to God in the highest, and on earth peace among those with whom he is pleased!" (Luke 2:14). When you believe in Jesus Christ for the salvation of your soul, you find the peace that surpasses understanding and inexpressible joy (Philippians 4:5–7).

Every day, when you and I wake up, we get to make a choice. We can choose each morning to think first of what pleases God, knowing that it is the way to freedom, or we can choose to go back to a form of people pleasing that is all about us. I'm going to have days, you're going to have days, when we slide back into old habits and old stories. The trails we carved with feet intent on chasing down validation or running away from feeling awkward, those are paths we slide down with familiarity. But I'm ready, and I think you are too, to live a better day, a better promise, to walk in a better way. There's a better prize when we put God first, when we love and care for others from an unselfish place, and when we let Jesus be our peace.

"His delight is not in the strength of the horse, nor his pleasure in the legs of a man," the Bible says in Psalm 147:10–11, "but the LORD takes pleasure in those who fear him, in those who hope in his steadfast love."

Peace and freedom to you, my friend. Far more than the approval of others, far beyond what you've run from, far better than the hurts you've experienced and the applause you've chased, may the freedom you find in Jesus fill your heart.

Let's Chat About It

Friend, as we wrap up our time together, I'm filled with so much hope for you. It's my prayer you walk closer and closer with Jesus. It's my prayer that you find a healthy, Bible-based church. I pray you find a community of people to love and serve. I pray you walk in freedom and peace.

> *For freedom Christ has set us free; stand firm therefore, and do not submit again to a yoke of slavery.*
> GALATIANS 5:1

ACKNOWLEDGMENTS

BEFORE ANYONE ELSE, I MUST ACKNOWLEDGE JULIE Lyles-Carr. Julie, you are a thoughtful friend, a fountain of wisdom, and an incredibly gifted writer. Thank you for the countless hours you poured into this project, helping me turn my thoughts into words on a page. I'd like you to know that you're extraordinary.

Bryan Norman, your vision for what this project could be both inspired and motivated me. Thanks for being a fun hang and the best agent in the business.

To Stephanie Newton, Carrie Marrs, Ashley Reed, Lauren Bridges, Caren Wolfe, Allison Carter, and the entire team at W Publishing Group: you are *the* dream team. Thank you for continuing to believe in me.

To my daughters, Felicity Nicole and Evangeline Jo: you are beautiful inside and out. I love you and so does Jesus.

Jeremy, when I married you, you promised to love me through the good times and the bad. Well, this book-writing process has had a bit of both and you continue to show me that you meant what you said. To express just how much I love you is impossible (though I think Julie could help me get close).

Ruth Chou Simons once wrote that "Our hope in the midst of hardship is that Jesus doesn't just work things out for our good—He is our good." It is to my Lord and Savior, Jesus Christ, who is my good, that I owe my greatest thanks. Because He loved me, I am free.

NOTES

CHAPTER 3
1. "4 Habits of 'SuperAgers,'" Northwestern Medicine, Northwestern Memorial HealthCare, updated October 2023, https://www.nm.org /healthbeat/healthy-tips/4-habits-super-agers.
2. "How Community Affects Wellbeing," Australian Unity, October 16, 2020, https://www.australianunity.com.au/wellbeing /What-is-real-wellbeing/How-community-affects-wellbeing.
3. "How Community Affects Wellbeing."
4. Olin Miller, "Olin Miller's Comment," *Reno Evening Gazette*, December 19, 1936.

CHAPTER 4
1. *Online Etymology Dictionary*, s.v. "desperate," accessed March 22, 2024, https://www.etymonline.com/search?q=desperate.

CHAPTER 6
1. Allison Kooser, "You Will Meet 80,000 People in Your Lifetime," Swell + Good, September 23, 2021, https://swellandgood.com /you-will-meet-80000-people-in-your-lifetime/.

2. *Thayer's Greek-English Lexicon*, s.v. "katakrinō," Blue Letter Bible, accessed December 30, 2023, https://www.blueletterbible.org /lexicon/g2632/kjv/tr/0–1/.

CHAPTER 7

1. Frederick Gome Cassidy and Joan Hall, eds., *Dictionary of American Regional English: I–O*, vol. 3 (Cambridge, MA: Harvard University Press, 1985), s.v. "Ole Ole Olson All In Free."

CHAPTER 8

1. Annabelle G.Y. Lim, "Big Five Personality Traits: The 5-Factor Model of Personality," Simply Psychology, updated December 20, 2023, https://www.simplypsychology.org/big-five-personality.html.
2. Charles Bridges, *Proverbs* (Wheaton, IL: Crossway, 2001), 234.

CHAPTER 9

1. "Don Stewart:: Who Were the Scribes?" Blue Letter Bible, accessed December 30, 2023, https://www.blueletterbible.org/faq /don_stewart/don_stewart_1315.cfm.
2. *Encyclopaedia Britannica Online*, s.v. "Scribes and Pharisees of Jesus," accessed December 30, 2023, https://www.britannica.com /biography/Jesus/Scribes-and-Pharisees.
3. Morgan Smith, "Burnout Is On the Rise Worldwide—and Gen Z, Young Millennials and Women Are the Most Stressed," CNBC, March 14, 2023, https://www.cnbc.com/2023/03/14/burnout-is-on -the-rise-gen-z-millennials-and-women-are-the-most-stressed.html.
4. Carly Thomas, "21 Actors Committed to Method Acting at Some Point in Their Career," *Hollywood Reporter*, August 13, 2023, https://www .hollywoodreporter.com/lists/actors-method-acting-prepare-roles/.
5. Jennifer Bustance, "Is Method Acting Dangerous?" *Backstage*, updated August 18, 2023, https://www.backstage.com/magazine /article/is-method-acting-dangerous-76443/.

CHAPTER 10

1. Allison Gatline, "Hospital Joins Study of Snakebite Treatment," *Antelope Valley Press*, June 6, 2023, https://www.avpress.com /news/hospital-joins-study-of-snakebite-treatment /article_410e91d2–0417–11ee-a644-eba47b40fc72.html.

2. *Strong's Greek Lexicon*, s.v. "ophthalmodoulia," Blue Letter Bible, accessed December 30, 2023, https://www.blueletterbible.org /lexicon/g3787/esv/mgnt/0–1/.

3. *Strong's Greek Lexicon*, s.v. "anthrōpareskos," Blue Letter Bible, accessed December 30, 2023, https://www.blueletterbible.org /lexicon/g441/esv/mgnt/0–1/.

CHAPTER 11

1. *Strong's Greek Lexicon,* s.v. "paraineō," Blue Letter Bible, accessed March 22, 2024, https://www.blueletterbible.org/lexicon/g3867 /kjv/tr/0–1/.

ABOUT THE AUTHOR

JINGER DUGGAR VUOLO grew up on TV. From the age of nine until twenty-seven, she appeared on her family's hit TLC reality shows, *19 Kids and Counting* and *Counting On*. She is an author whose books include *New York Times* bestseller *Becoming Free Indeed*; her personal memoir *The Hope We Hold*; and a children's book, *You Can Shine So Bright*. She now lives in Los Angeles with her husband, Jeremy, and their two daughters, Felicity Nicole and Evangeline Jo. In her free time, Jinger enjoys traveling, hiking, and anything to do with good food.